Keyboard Results
Piano and Fundamentals for Everyone
Volume 1

First Edition

Jay Snyder
Glendale Community College

© 2008, 2010, 2011 by Jay Snyder
All rights reserved

Printed in the United States of America
Published by Golden Retriever Media

ISBN – 978-0-578-08110-6

Credits:

Sibelius/Compositor	Tim Helisek
Permissions and Clearances	Marcus Thomas, Esq.
Illustrator	Carlos Nieto III
Flash Cards	Arnaud Damesceno
Website and Marketing	Younger Hong
Cover Design	Scott Ford

Unmarked pieces were written and/or arranged by the author.

Reference within this text to any specific commercial or non-commercial product, process, or service by trade name, trademark, manufacturer or otherwise does not constitute or imply an endorsement, recommendation, or favoring by the author.

The views and opinions of the author do not necessarily state or reflect the opinions of the product owners, and cannot be used for advertising or product endorsement purposes.

References to books, software, Web sites, or products as "Recommended by Jay Snyder" are specific suggestions only and do not necessarily constitute or imply an endorsement.

All service marks, trade names and trademarks used herein are for illustrative purposes only and remain the exclusive property of their respective owners.

Contents

Preface vi
Introduction vii

Chapter 1

Getting Started 1
The Staff 2
How to Find Middle C 2
Duration Symbols 3
The Beat 4
Time Signature 4
Counting 5
Goal: 30 Notes - A Few at a Time 6
Seating and Hand Position 7
Five Treble Clef Notes 7
Octaves 11
Five Bass Clef Notes 11
The Grand Staff 15
How to Practice 21
Why Acquire Piano Skills? 21
Rhythm Gym 22
Questions 23
Guided Practice 23
Music for Sight Reading and Practice 26

Chapter 2

Memory Check 32
New Notes: Treble Clef 32
New Duration Symbol: Dotted Half 36
New Notes: Bass Clef 38
Why Learn Fundamentals? 40
Components of a Major Scale 40
    Major and Minor Seconds, Half Steps and Whole Steps
How to Construct a Major Scale 41
Thumb Under 42
Rhythm Gym 44
Questions 45
Guided Practice: C Major Scale - Hands Separately, C Major Scale - Hands Together 46
Music for Sight Reading and Practice 47

Chapter 3

Memory Check 52
New Notes: Treble Clef 52
New Notes: Bass Clef 58
Chromatic 63
New Scale: G 66
New Scale: F 74
Stem Direction 78
Definitions & Symbols: Ties, Rests, and Repeat Signs 79
Anacrusis 81
New Time Signature: 3/4 82
New Intervals: Minor and Major Thirds 87
Why Study Chords? 88
Where Do Chords Come From? 88
Tessitura and Transposition, Part I 90
Nashville Number System 94
Rhythm Gym 95
Questions 97
Guided Practice: Principles of Fingering 98
Music for Sight Reading and Practice 100

Chapter 4

Memory Check 105
New Notes: Treble Clef 105
New Notes: Bass Clef 108
New Duration Symbols: Eighth Note and Rest, Dotted Quarter and Rest 110
Beaming 112
Bass and Melody Lines from Bach Chorales 115
Interval Review 121
New Intervals: Perfect Fourth and Perfect Fifth, Augmented Fourth/Diminished Fifth 122
The Circle of Fifths 123
Enharmonics, Part I 126
Sachiyo's Tunes 127
New Scales: D and B♭ 127
Bonus Notes 134
Simple and Compound Meter 139
Chords So Far 146
Rhythm Gym 151
Questions 152
Guided Practice: Unchained Melody 153
Music for Sight Reading and Practice 156

Appendix 1: Scales and Primary Triads 161

Appendix 2: More Examples of Time Signatures 180

Glossary 182

Index 196

Flash Cards

Preface to Volume 1

Welcome to KEYBOARD RESULTS: Piano and Fundamentals for Everyone.

How does it work? VERY SLOWLY.

Learning to read piano music is similar to learning to read a foreign language. First, you learn the alphabet; this is where other methods make things difficult if they go too fast, expecting too much too soon. KEYBOARD RESULTS makes sure you're totally confident with a few notes before new ones are introduced.

What about the fundamentals or theory component of KEYBOARD RESULTS?

You'll find this book moves from piano to fundamentals and back to piano in a logical, information-as-needed fashion. Sometimes it takes a few pages to explain a bit about music theory. For those who would rather just stick to learning piano, you're free to skip to the next keyboard component.

A new teaching technique in KEYBOARD RESULTS is called 'Guided Practice;' it's like having a teacher or musical friend sitting there next to you, explaining things, step-by-step.

Volume 1 of KEYBOARD RESULTS familiarizes you with 30 notes, common major chords, and basic sight reading skills so you can play some popular songs and simple classical music. If you'd like to learn more, Volume 2 takes you to a more advanced level.

Have fun!

js

Introduction

You are about to become linked to an ancient tradition – making music. Your ancestors are people like Bach, Beethoven, and Billy Preston as well as the anonymous keyboard player in a chamber group entertaining royalty. And like your ancestors, once you've learned the names of the notes and where they go on a piece of paper, you will possess a great power; you'll be able to *make music*.

How much you learn and what you do with that knowledge is up to you. With a handful of chords and the ability to keep a steady beat you could wind up in the Rock and Roll Hall of Fame. After years of practice and perseverance, you could be performing on the stage of Carnegie Hall. Maybe you'll touch the lives of thousands, even millions of people, or maybe you'll just bring back a memory and a smile with a song or melody you play for just one person. However you apply what you're about to learn in music, it will most likely be a positive force in the world, and that can only be good.

CHAPTER ONE

Getting Started

The two most basic elements of piano music are rhythm and pitch. Rhythmic units express durations - how long a sound lasts. Pitch expresses highness or lowness of sound.

Sit in front of a piano or keyboard. A piano will have a logo or name like Yamaha or Steinway in the middle. That name helps you find the center of the instrument.

Without worrying about a right way or wrong way to do this, just put your fingers on the keys, press down, make some sound and enjoy the results. Have your hands go all over the keyboard. Notice that as you play white or black keys to the right, the sound gets higher, and as you play keys or notes to the left, sounds get lower.

These high and low sounds are called PITCHES. The **white notes** on the piano express these pitches using the first seven letters of the English alphabet:

A B C D E F G

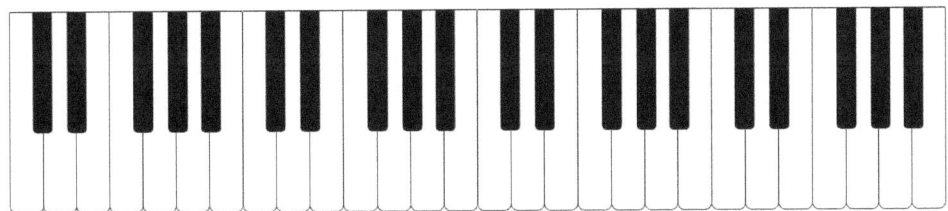

The **black keys** are grouped by 2's and 3's, help orient us to the white notes of the keyboard, and are named in relation to the white notes. For our purposes, we'll call them 'Black Group 2' and 'Black Group 3.'

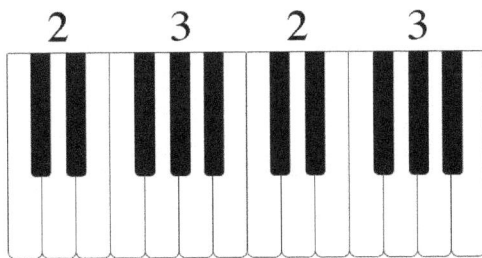

The Staff

To express the highness or lowness of a pitch, we need a grid of some sort, a place to put notes. That grid is called a STAFF and looks like this.

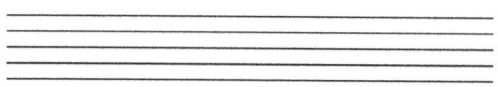

To give this staff a point of reference - what note names of the alphabet these lines and spaces represent - a symbol called a TREBLE CLEF is used. It's also called a G CLEF because when this symbol is placed on a staff, the second curly line to the right stops on the note G. By doing this we are saying that second line from the bottom is a G.

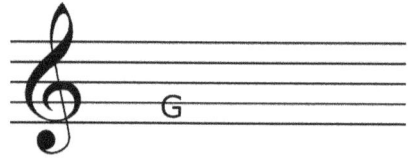

Here's the big picture.

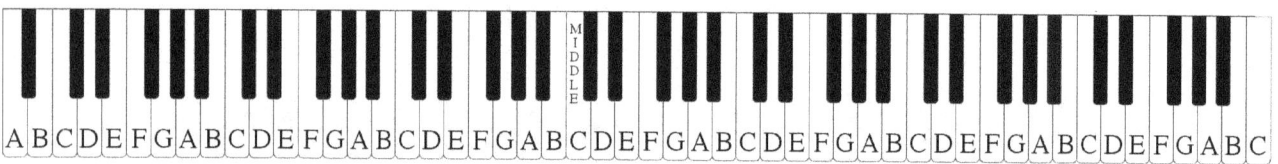

We orient ourselves to the piano keyboard with a note called MIDDLE C. Just as its name implies, middle C is right in the middle of the piano keyboard.

How to find middle C

- Make sure you're sitting in front of the piano's logo.

- Find the centermost grouping of two black keys and choose the black key to the left.

- From that black key, slide left, down to the nearest white key. That note is middle C.

And where is middle C on the staff? It's not on the staff!

The staff holds nine notes on five lines and four spaces plus the notes that sit on the top and bottom of the staff. That makes eleven notes.

In order to write the note called middle C and notes other than the eleven that sit on the five lines and four spaces, we have to extend the staff. This is done with what is called a LEDGER LINE. Ledger lines allow us to indicate notes that are above or below the staff. Since middle C is below the staff here is how it looks.

Middle C

Duration Symbols

One of the elegant things about music is that its symbols combine the information for both pitch and duration. You've seen how pitches placed on the staff reveal highness or lowness. Now look at how some of these symbols or notes indicate how long to hold that note.

♩ = 1 Beat = Quarter note

𝅗𝅥 = 2 Beats = Half note

𝅝 = 4 Beats = Whole Note

The Beat

Like the relative steadiness of a heartbeat, music has an underlying, even pulse called THE BEAT. One of the simplest and most common beats consists of 4 pulses that repeat over and over again. You hear it in rock, rap, R&B, disco, gospel, blues, electronica, marches, and symphonies. A beat with pitches equals some basic music.

Because this beat keeps repeating 1-2-3-4, 1-2-3-4 we have to subdivide the staff into short sections to visually represent the 1-2-3-4 groupings. These sections are called MEASURES or BARS. Vertical lines create BAR LINES.

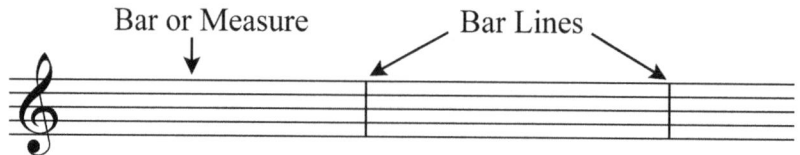

Time Signature

So that we can write some real music using the beat, let's introduce the idea of what is called a TIME SIGNATURE. We'll start with this simplest and most common time signature called FOUR FOUR TIME. It's written like this: $\frac{4}{4}$ and is placed to the right of the treble clef sign. It imparts this information:

- Top number = How many beats are in a measure

  (In this case there are four beats in every measure)

- Bottom number = What kind of a note gets one beat

(Helpful hint: Cover up the top number and pretend there's a number 1 there. This means a 1/4 or a quarter note gets one of those 4 beats detailed in the top number.)

Counting

One of the big secrets in learning how to read music is counting. Counting helps you keep your place and stay in time (keep the beat steady). In the case of 4/4 time, all you have to do is count to four, over and over.

If you have all quarter notes in a bar, you will hit a note on the piano for every number you say. Count 1-2-3-4 and play note-note-note-note.

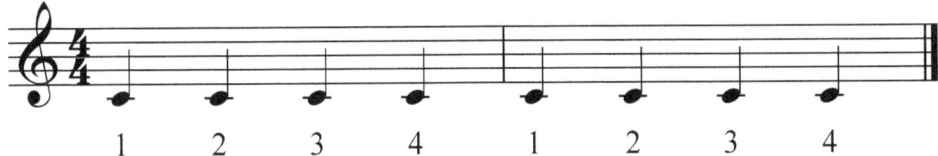

If you have a whole note in a bar, count **1-2-3-4**, play the note on count one and hold your finger down while you finish counting 2-3-4.

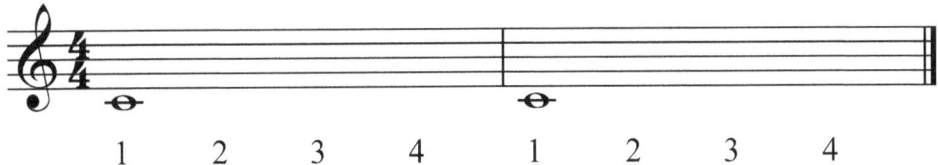

If you have a half note, it gets 2 counts or 2 beats. Two half notes in a bar would count like this: **1**-2-**3**-4. Play the note on beat 1, hold for beat 2. Play the note on beat 3, hold for beat 4.

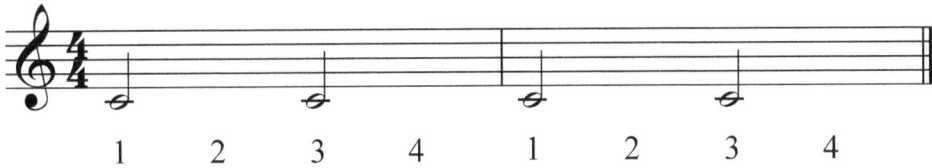

Since we only know one note so far - middle C - here is the rhythm (almost) to Jingle Bells. Underlining shows the duration of the note.

Almost Jingle Bells

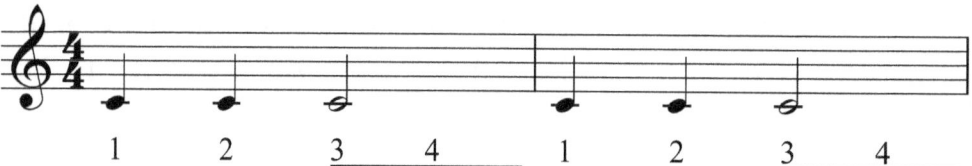

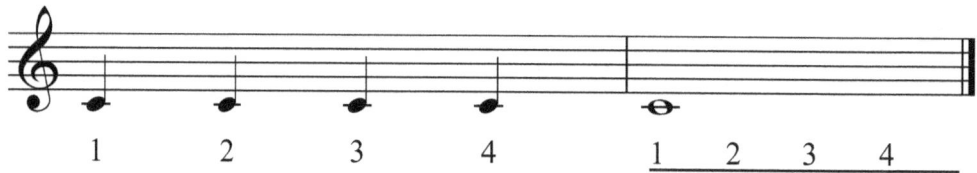

Goal: 30 Notes - A Few At A Time

When you begin a new project or set out to learn something new, it helps to set short-term and long-term goals. The short-term goal in this book for pitches is approximately 30 notes – 15 notes in the treble clef

and 15 notes in the bass clef.

The English alphabet has 26 letters so 30 symbols is not so much to ask to learn the language of music. There are, of course, more notes, but 30 will give you the ability to play a wide variety of repertoire and styles.

To begin with you're going to learn 5 notes for the right hand and 5 notes for the left hand. But before you do that let's get serious about how to sit at the keyboard and what to do with your hand.

Seating and hand position

- Sit up straight with your feet on the floor in front of the piano pedals
- Your elbows should be at the same level or slightly above the keyboard
- Your palm is shaped as if it were covering a ping pong ball
- Your fingers are curved
- Put your right thumb on the note middle C; put the other 4 fingers on the next 4 white keys
- Your wrist should feel loose and relaxed
- Press the individual keys down with your fingers and try not to force the keys down using your wrist or arm

Five Treble Clef Notes

Keeping in mind the alphabet, here are the first five notes of the treble clef to learn starting on middle C.

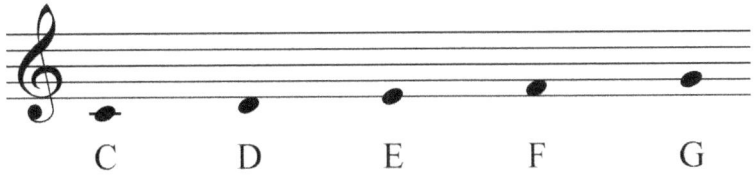

How you learn these notes is up to you and your learning style (visual, aural, touching). Here are some of the things you may want to notice to help you learn, followed by some music in the treble clef for you to practice.

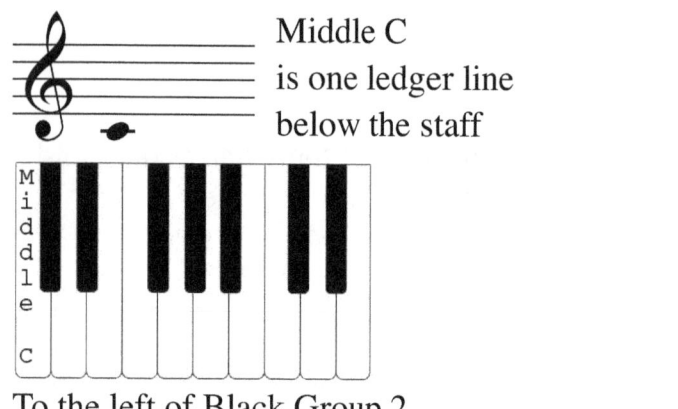

Middle C is one ledger line below the staff

To the left of Black Group 2

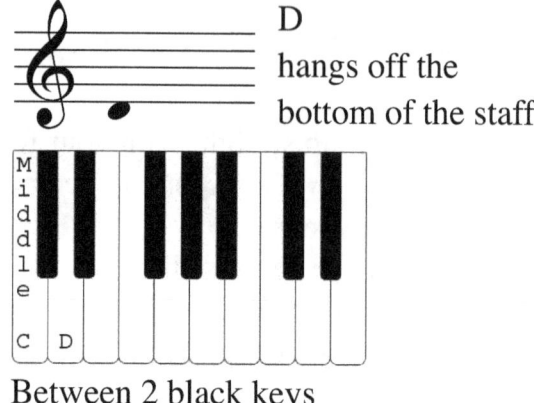

D hangs off the bottom of the staff

Between 2 black keys of Black Group 2

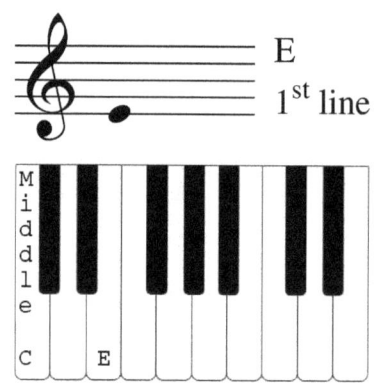

E
1st line

To the right of Black Group 2

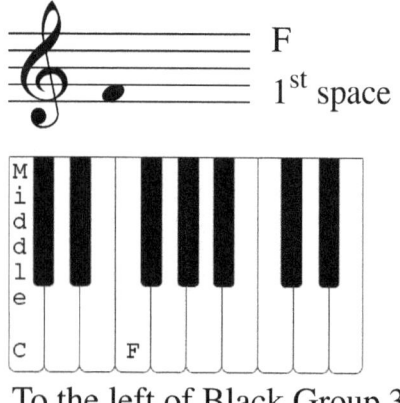

F
1st space

To the left of Black Group 3

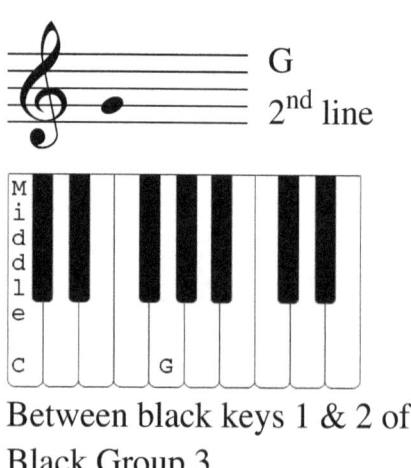

G
2nd line

Between black keys 1 & 2 of Black Group 3

Here are some exercises to help you learn C-D-E-F-G.
<u>Fingering</u> - what finger goes with what note - is indicated above the note by the numbers 1 (thumb), 2, 3, 4 or 5.

Octaves

When you looked at the entire piano keyboard, you saw that there were many C's, many D's etc. A note that is exactly 8 notes above or below another is called an OCTAVE. The Italian word is 'ottava.' 8 notes below middle C is an octave of C. 8 notes higher than middle C is also an octave of C. This applies to all notes; they all have octaves.

Five Bass Clef Notes

One octave below middle C is an octave of C. If we tried to write this note using the treble clef it would look like this with many ledger lines:

So that we would have an easier way to write this note and others in this area or range, there is another clef called the BASS CLEF.

Just as the treble clef defined the staff by pointing out the note G on the second line from the bottom, so does the bass clef do the same thing in pointing out the reference note F by surrounding the fourth line from the bottom with two dots.

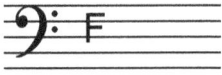

Here is how the notes C D E F G look on the bass clef one octave below middle C.

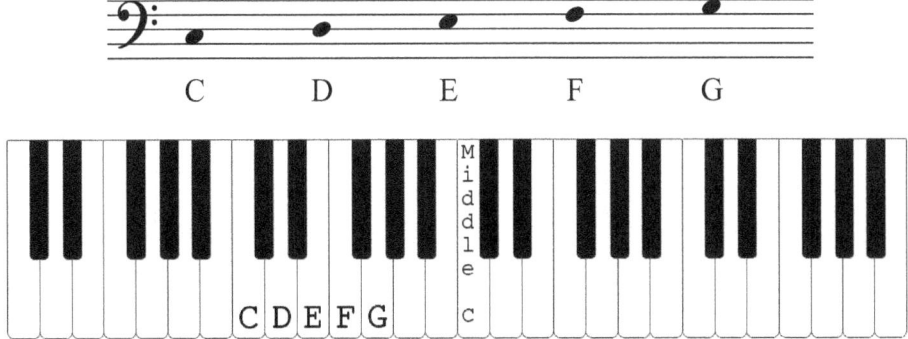

This is how these notes look separately. After you've learned these notes, practice reading bass clef music on the following pages.

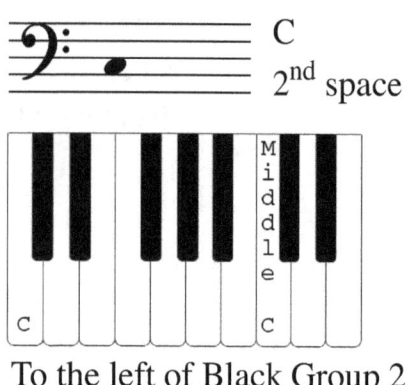

C
2nd space

To the left of Black Group 2

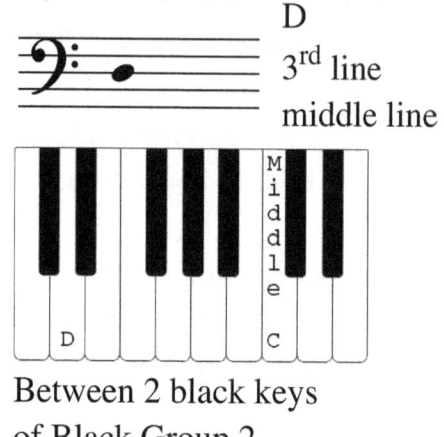

D
3rd line
middle line

Between 2 black keys
of Black Group 2

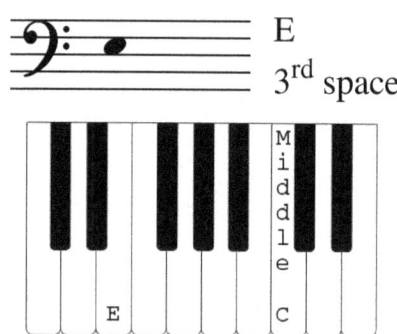

E
3rd space

To the right of Black Group 2

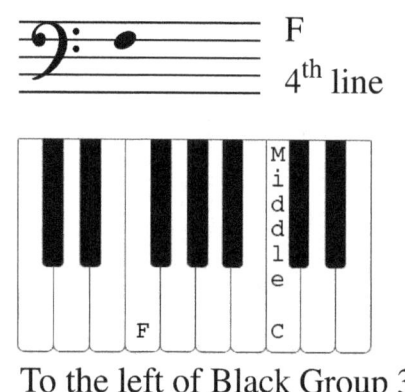

F
4th line

To the left of Black Group 3

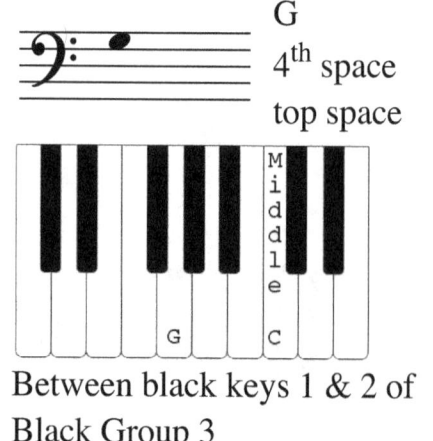

G
4th space
top space

Between black keys 1 & 2 of
Black Group 3

More Bass Clef C-D-E-F-G

The Grand Staff

In piano music, the treble clef and bass clef normally appear together linked by a brace. This whole thing is called the GRAND STAFF.

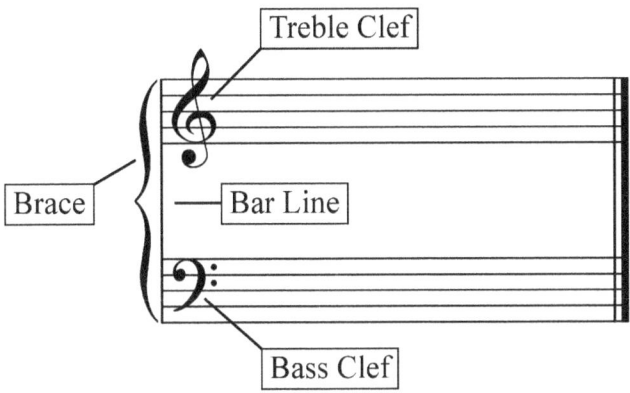

Having learned five notes in the treble clef and five notes in the bass clef, it's time to read the two clefs at the same time. This can be a mind blowing, frustrating experience for some. And yet millions of pianists through the centuries have come through this process and learned to read piano music.

One of the keys to reading the grand staff is to *go very slowly at first*. Let you mind/brain take in this newly learned information and process it at whatever speed it needs to. The biggest mistake beginners make is to try to play things too fast. Whatever music you practice or play should be at a pace you can manage so the music doesn't slow down or speed up.

What follows is music written for the piano using the grand staff. By the time you are done practicing this music, you should have total confidence in the 10 notes or pitches of the right and left hand, and be comfortable playing $\frac{4}{4}$ time using quarter, half and whole notes.

1.
2.
3.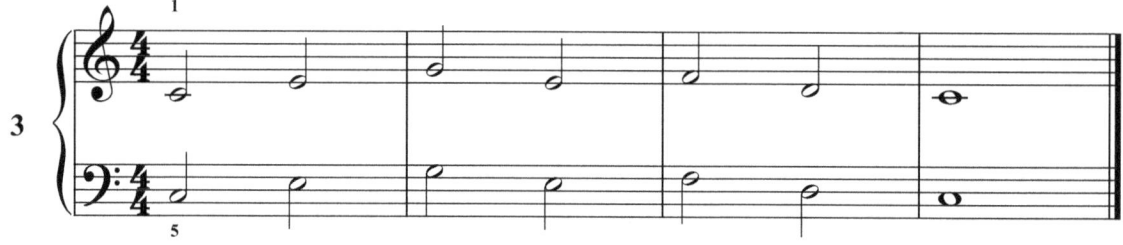
4.
5.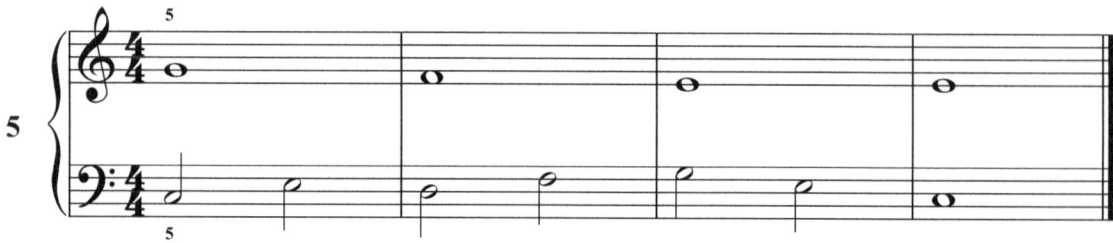

1

2

3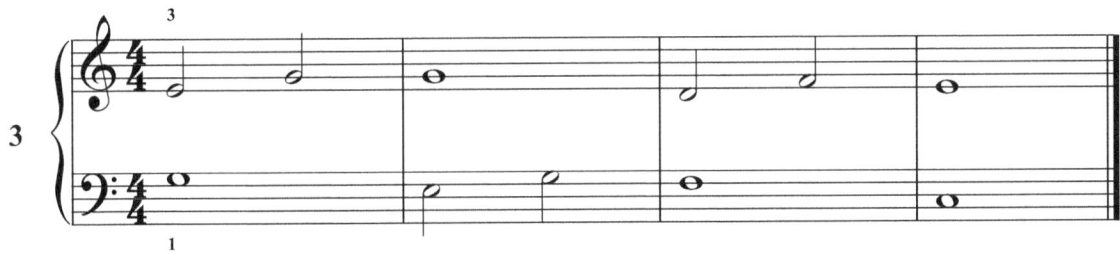

4

5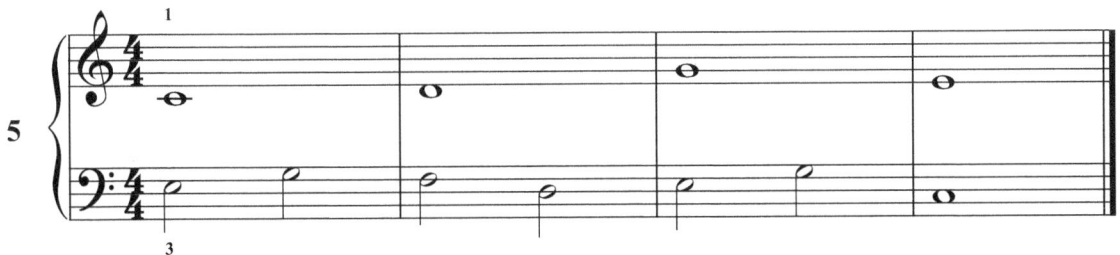

Ten Note Goal

How To Practice

Using the proper methods when you practice will lead to success.

- Allot enough time. 45 minutes is a good, reasonable amount.
- Sit correctly and keep your wrists loose.
- Warm up first. Beginners use 5 consecutive notes called pentachords, then go on to other patterns.
- When learning a new piece of music, take each hand separately. It's your choice whether you practice bass or treble clef first. Then, put the hands together and play slowly.
- Practice in one or two bar segments, then link sections. Starting at the beginning and playing all the way to the end, making the same mistakes over and over, is the worst way to practice and accomplishes very little.
- Use the same fingering each time you play the piece. You are building muscle memory.
- Shake your wrists and shoulders if they get stiff or sore. Take a break.

Why Acquire Piano Skills?

Are you enjoying yourself so far? If the answer is 'yes' then good. If the answer is 'no,' do you want to quit? Either way you might want to reflect for a moment on your long-term goal because the ability to play the piano opens a world of many possibilities to you.

- Strengthens perseverance and self-discipline
- Gives you the ability to entertain yourself and others
- Enables you to write a song using the piano
- Enables you to write music using the piano
- Playing all styles of music is possible: Rock, Blues, Jazz, Classical
- Makes possible a career or an auxiliary income as a musician, accompanist, choir director, songwriter, rock star, teacher, musical director
- Achieving a level of competence is satisfying

Rhythm Gym

If you were a weight lifter who wanted to increase upper body strength, you'd do a series of exercises designed to work particular muscle groups. Rhythm Gym does the same thing; it gets you used to seeing certain rhythms without pitches so you can concentrate on just the rhythm.

To get the most out of these exercises, count out loud, tap or say 'dah' as you do them. For example: 2 half notes in a bar would be dah, dah.

Questions

Q: How much do I need to practice?

A: Twenty minutes a day produces minimal, average results. Your hands will feel sluggish and won't be able to execute what your brain tells you. Forty-five minutes per day 5 to 6 days per week gives a better result and an hour a day usually produces very good results if you practice correctly i.e. slowly and with thought. Occasionally, when you're working towards a breakthrough, you may get into a mental space where you don't notice time passing. Practice sessions like these produce a lot of progress and fabulous results.

Q: What's up with 'Every Good Boy Deserves Fudge?'

A: This is an old mnemonic (memory) device that some people find useful in learning the names of the notes. Other people find it a lifelong burden and always have to step through the acronym in their minds. For example: to find D, this person climbs the lines of the treble clef and thinks Every Good Boy Deserves. D!!! That's too much thinking to go through every time you see a note. It's like having a middleman in your head. A better result comes from practicing with flash cards - included for free at the end of this book.

Q: What do sharps and flats mean?

A: For now - a sharp (♯) raises a note's pitch; a flat (♭) lowers a note's pitch.

Guided Practice

This feature of the text is like having a teacher or tutor sitting next to you as you practice a particular piece of music. Fingerings, hand movements (if there are any), trouble spots, all things musically related to the piece are discussed. Today's Guided Practice is an eight bar piece based around the idea of a pentachord. A pentachord is a five-note span of notes - no more, no less. Pentachords are useful in developing finger strength and hand-eye coordination. Since the fingering for a pentachord is different from a scale, it's not a good idea to dwell on them, but for starters they're fine.

Guided Practice #1

1. Start with the left hand. Place your 5th finger (little finger) on the C below middle C. Why? Because the span of notes in the left hand is from C to G. Five consecutive notes on white keys in the bass will usually take the fingering 5-4-3-2-1 for C-D-E-F-G.

2. You've been working on memorizing C-D-E-F-G in the bass clef. Now apply it. Play the 8 bars. Did you encounter any tricky spots? At bar 5, did you want to play a G instead of a C?

One of the tricks of reading music is to look ahead. That means, for example, while your mind has taken in the notes of bar 4 and is playing them, your eye has skipped forward to bar 5 and sees that both the left and right hand start with C's.

3. Bar 6 of the bass clef is different. Instead of being like previous bars with consecutive notes C-D-E-F, this bar has a pattern of skipping every other note: G-E-C-E. Notice the shape of that pattern on the staff: space-space-space-space. Here's another way to visualize it:

Recognizing shapes will help you read music better.

4. When the left hand is learned, play through the right hand. The same principle of 5 consecutive notes is at work. The span is from middle C to G so for C-D-E-F-G you will use the fingering 1-2-3-4-5.

Notice the shapes. In bars 1/2 and 3/4 the shape is ╱ . The white notes go up in order (line-space-line-space-line). In bars 7/8 the shape is ╲ . The white notes go down in order (line-space-line-space-line).

5. Time to put both hands together. If you have problems, go back to the treble clef and/or bass clef pages and concentrate on the notes. Don't write note names on this music. It won't help you learn to read in the long run. Work with the flash cards.

Look at bar 1. The right hand does most of the work; the left hand has only one note so your eye should go to where the most notes are. For the 8 bars of music, this is your eye path:

A quick glance at the whole notes should be all you need. If that glance is not enough to tell you what note you just saw, again, go back to the treble or bass clef pages and concentrate on learning those notes.

6. Slowly, play both hands. If you make a mistake somewhere – stop, analyze the problem, fix it, play that bar or bars until they're right, then go back to the beginning and play the whole piece.

7. Good job!

Music for Sight Reading and Practice

Any time you read a piece of music for the first time you are sight reading. Keeping a steady beat in mind, you simply look at a piece of music and play it without stopping. Sight reading is a valuable ability in music.

What follows are several pages of music for you to sight read. Playing a piece more than once would be considered practicing.

Music for Sight Reading and Practice

Octaves In Order

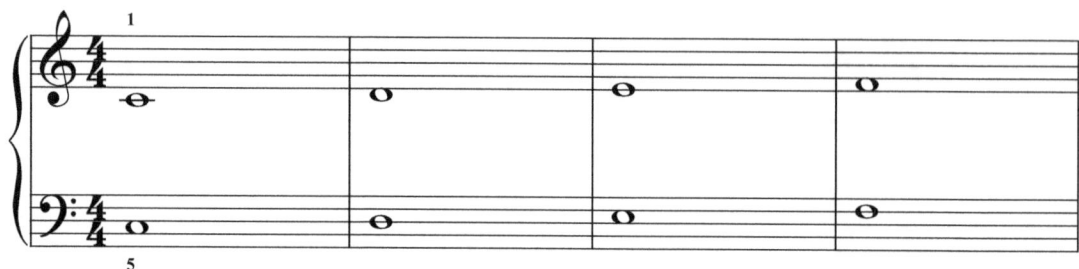

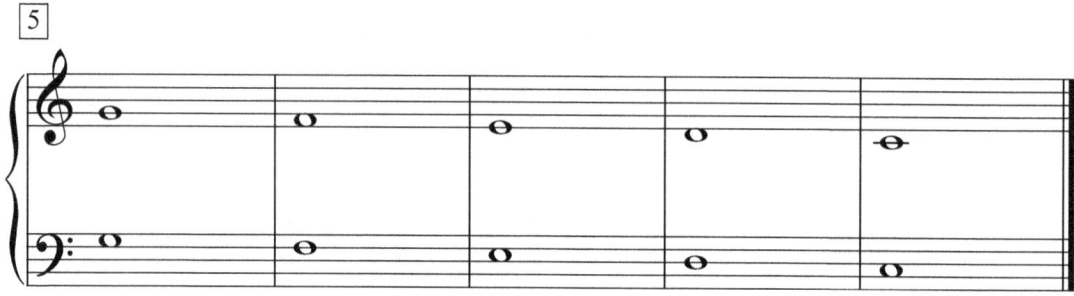

Octaves Out Of Order

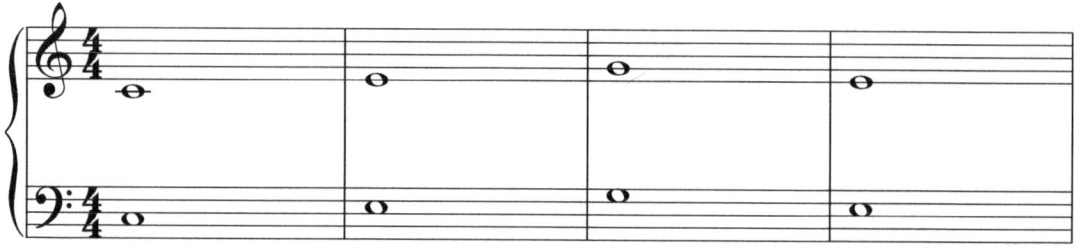

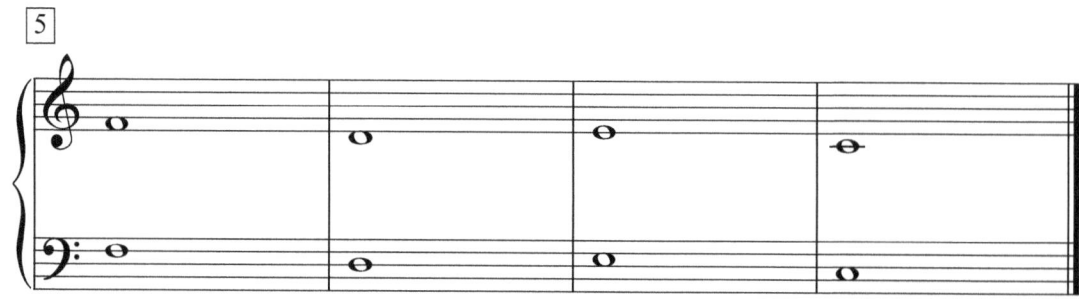

Next To Each Other

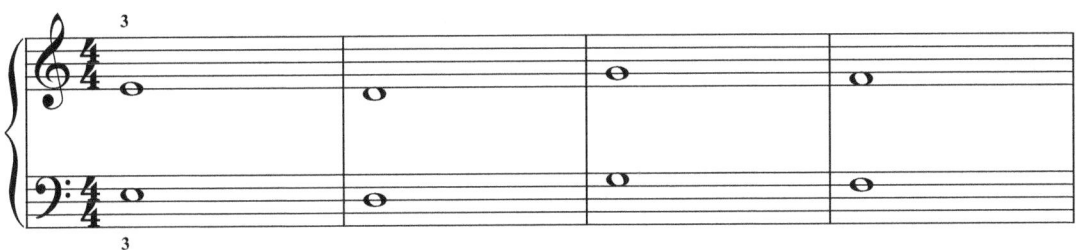

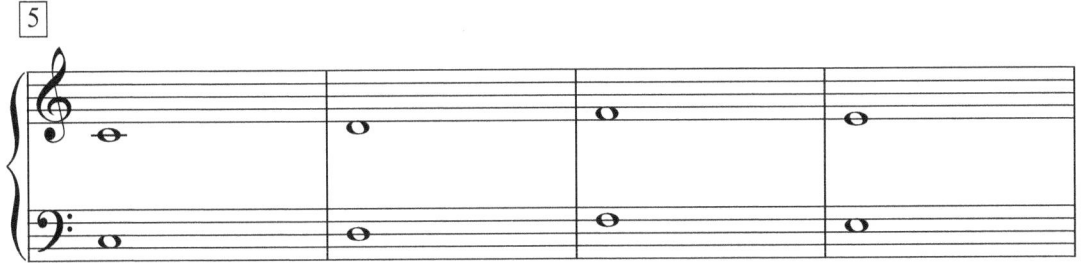

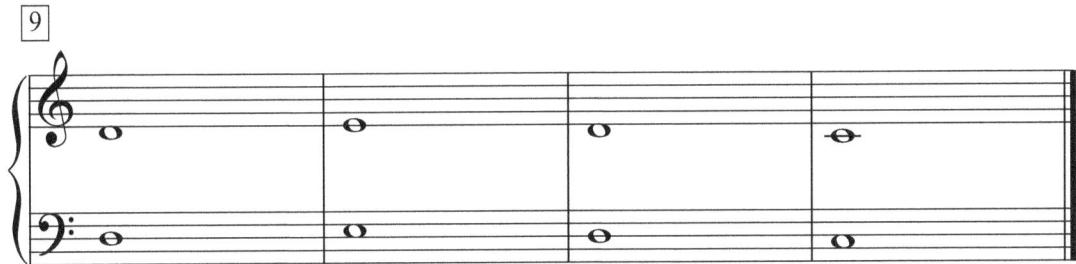

Different

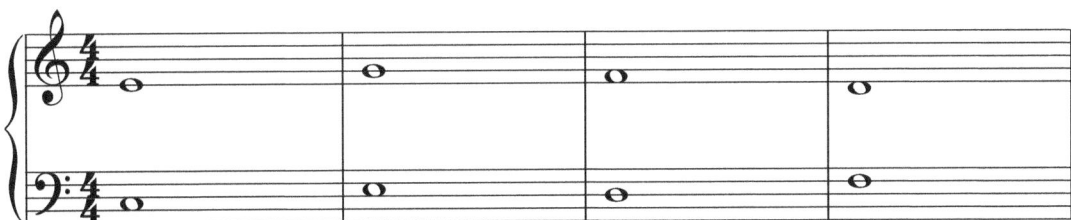

More Different

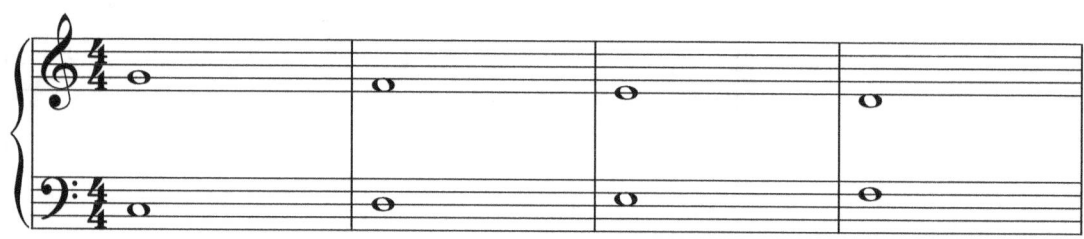
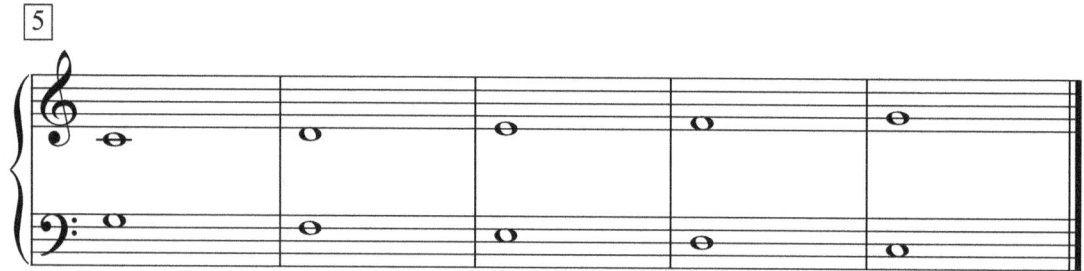

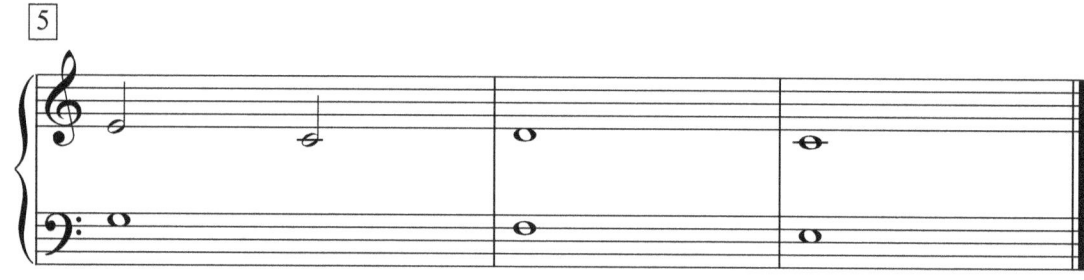

31

CHAPTER TWO

Memory Check

By now you should be completely familiar with these notes:

If you're not, review chapter one. Once you know these notes, read on.

New Notes: Treble Clef

Following the notes C-D-E-F-G upward are A-B-C. On the staff they look like this:

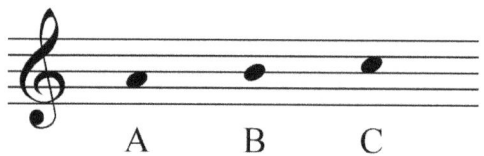

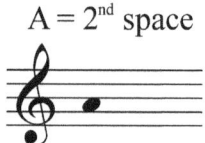

A = 2nd space

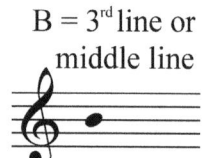

B = 3rd line or middle line

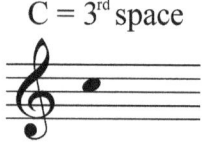

C = 3rd space

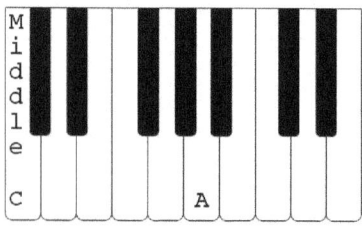

A is to the right of G, to the left of B

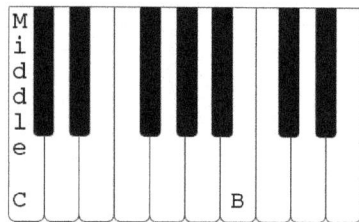

B is to the right of Black Group 3, to the left of C

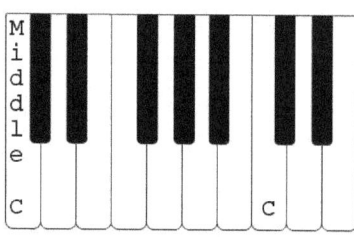

C is to the right of B, to the left of Black Group 2

It's very important to notice that

this C

and middle C

are in different parts of the keyboard and should not be mixed up.

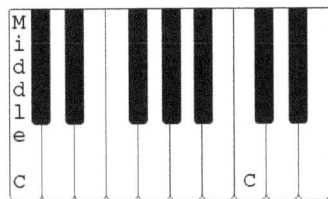

Here's a short exercise to help you remember the difference. In film and TV this trick has been used to suggest the passage of time or the ticking of a clock.

Use the following short exercises to reinforce A-B-C. Then go on to the combinations of C-D-E-F-G-A-B-C.

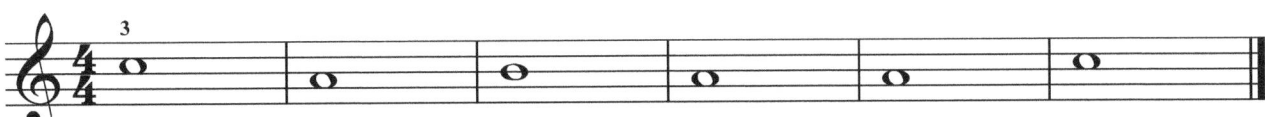

New Duration Symbol: Dotted Half

So far, we've worked with three duration symbols.

♩ = 1 Beat = Quarter note

𝅗𝅥 = 2 Beats = Half note

𝅝 = 4 Beats = Whole Note

In order to express 3 beats, we have this: 𝅗𝅥.
A half note with a dot to the right. It's called a DOTTED HALF.

Putting a dot next to any note adds half the value to the total number of beats.

𝅗𝅥 = 2   • = 1/2 of 2 or 1   𝅗𝅥• 2+1 = 3 beats

Likewise, if we put a dot next to a whole note

𝅝• = 6 beats (4 + 2 = 6)

Count out loud as you play the following piece

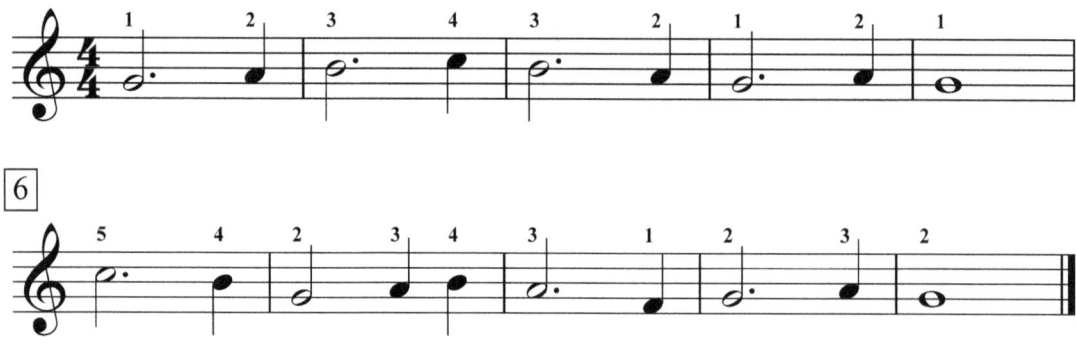

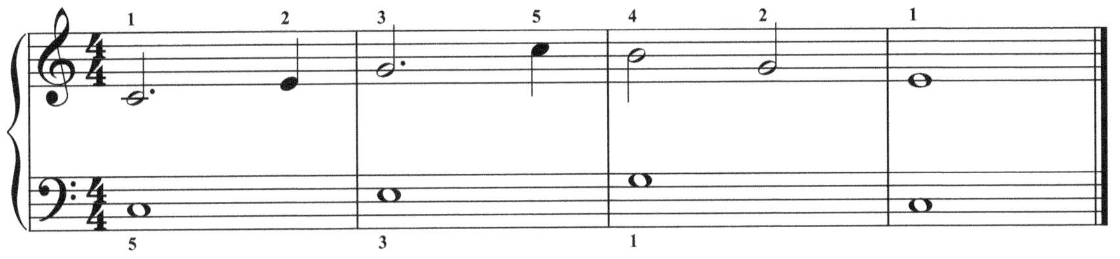

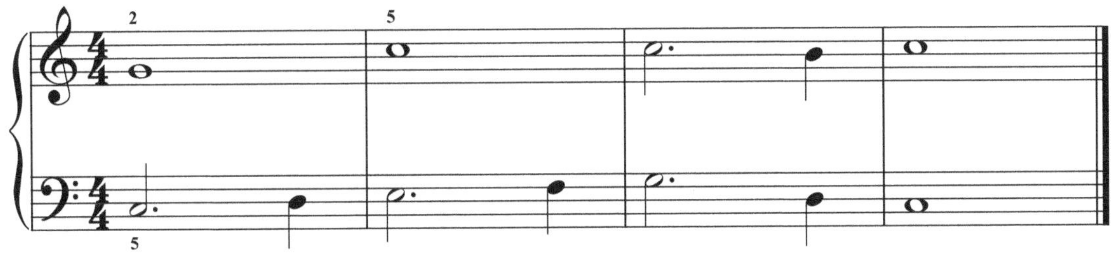

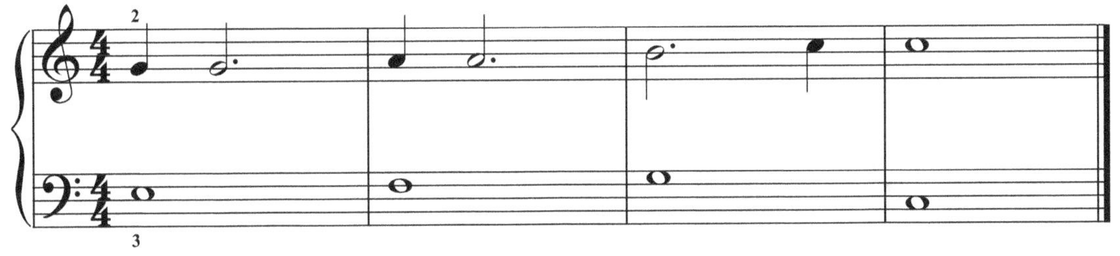

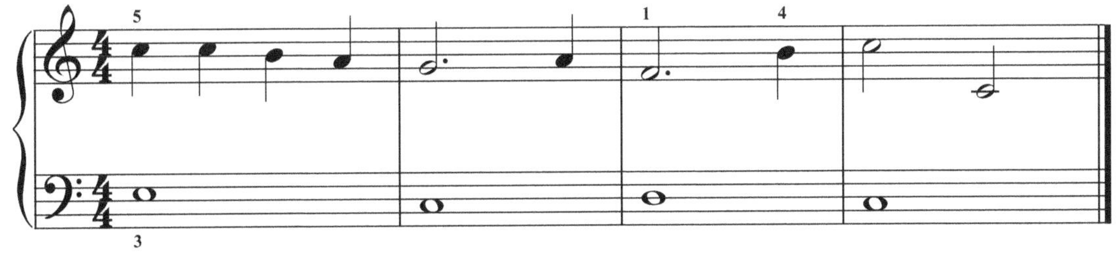

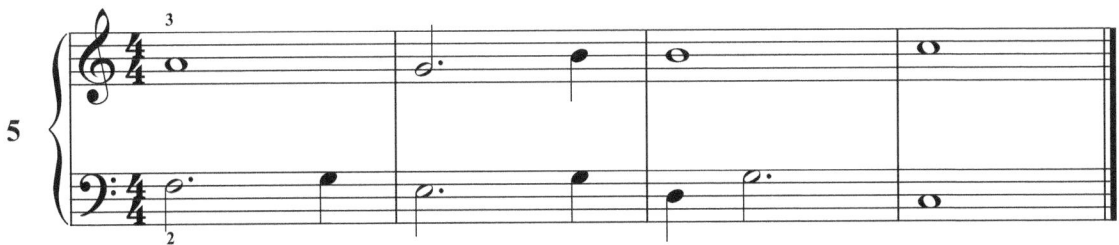

New Notes: Bass Clef

Following C-D-E-F-G in the bass clef are A-B-C.

On the staff these notes look like this:

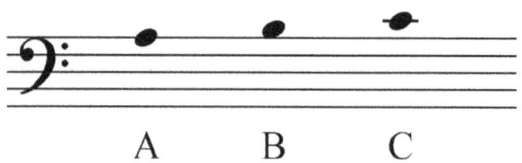

A   B   C

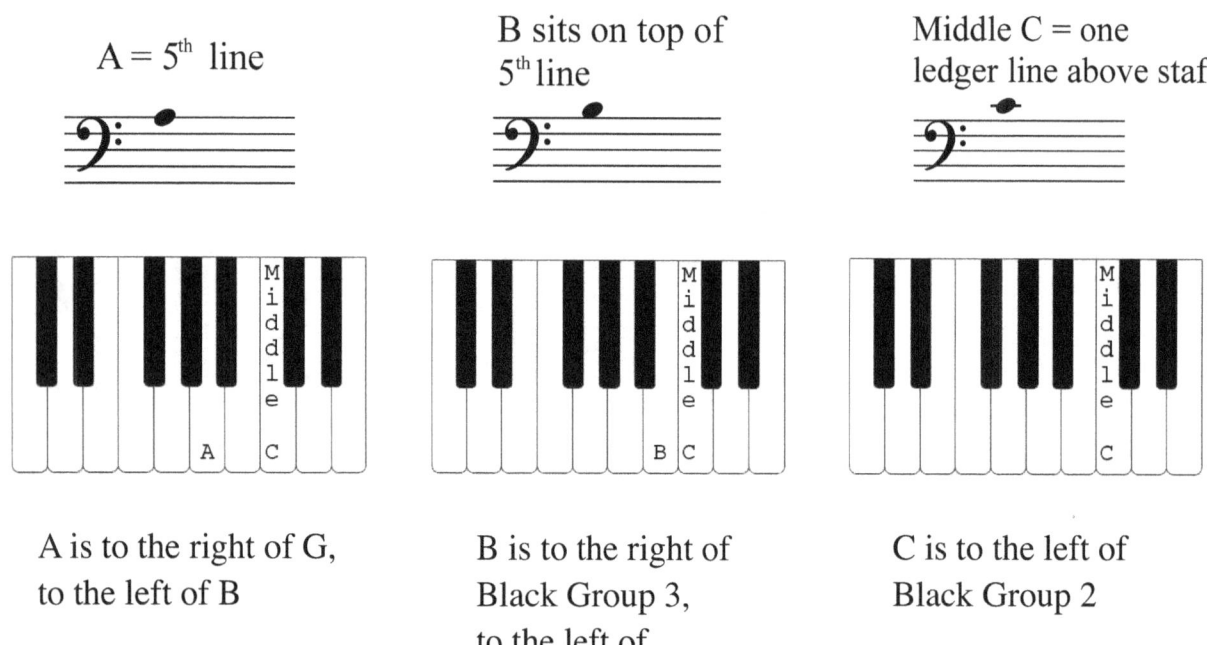

A = 5th line	B sits on top of 5th line	Middle C = one ledger line above staff
A is to the right of G, to the left of B	B is to the right of Black Group 3, to the left of middle C	C is to the left of Black Group 2

First play the exercises that help lock in A-B-C on the following page. Then add the exercises that cover all the bass notes so far: C-D-E-F-G-A-B-C.

Why Learn Fundamentals?

To understand the theory or fundamentals behind a subject is to be able to answer the many 'whys' that come up along the way of learning about something new. By learning about music fundamentals as you learn to play the piano, you'll gain an understanding of *what* you're playing. In the case of scales, knowing theory gives you the ability to think out any major scale in any key rather than reading it from preprinted music. Step one in learning fundamentals will be to look at the components that make up a major scale.

Components of the Major Scale

The distance from one thing to another is called an INTERVAL. The interval from the left side of this page to the right is 8 1/2 inches. The same is true of the distance between notes. A major scale is made up of intervals.

In music the smallest distances we work with on the piano are called SECONDS – MINOR SECONDS AND MAJOR SECONDS.

From E to F or from F to F♯ is called a minor second and is written like this.

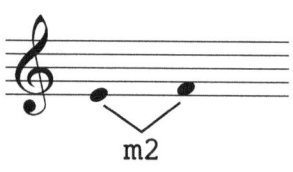
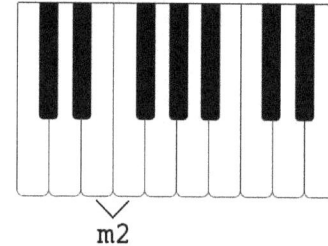

From E to F♯ or G♯ to A♯ is called a major second and is written like this.

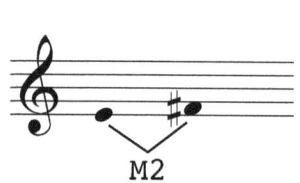
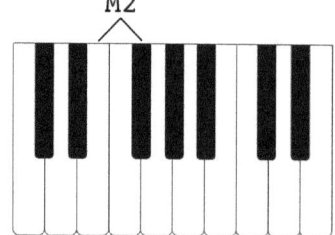

Notice that 2 consecutive minor seconds = a major second. Major and minor seconds also have other names and designations.

> Major 2nd = M2 = Whole step = W = Whole tone = 1
> minor 2nd = m2 = Half step = H = Half tone = Semi tone = 1/2

How to Construct a Major Scale

A SCALE is an ordered series of tones.

The formula (order of tones) for a major scale is:

WHOLE WHOLE HALF WHOLE WHOLE WHOLE HALF

If we want to construct a C major scale, we simply apply the formula.

C to D	D to E	E to F	F to G	G to A	A to B	B to C
W	W	H	W	W	W	H
1	1	1/2	1	1	1	1/2
M2	M2	m2	M2	M2	M2	m2

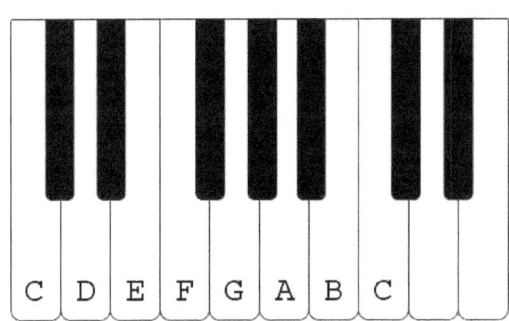

Major scale of C

Thumb Under

If every piece of music we played at the piano was based on a pentachord, we'd never have to worry about fingering. Everything would be 1-2-3-4-5. But most music encompasses more than five notes so we have to figure out a smooth way to go from note to note.

To go up and down an octave's worth of notes requires us to use a fingering principle called THUMB UNDER. If you try to play this with 1-2-3-4-5,

you'll run out of fingers with which to play the last three notes A-B-C. It's like backing yourself into a corner with nowhere to go, no options, no way out!

Here's how 'thumb under' works.

- Play the first three notes C-D-E with fingers 1-2-3

- Once your thumb has done its work and played C, it snaps to the right and waits while D and E are played

- It is then in place to play F as your 2nd finger brings the whole hand around to complete the scale with G-A-B-C or 2-3-4-5

To go *down* the C scale with the right hand, the first part is easy: 5-4-3-2-1.

Then your 3rd finger swings over to play E. 2-1, D-C finishes the scale.

The left hand fingering for the C scale is different.

C-D-E-F-G is as easy as 5-4-3-2-1, exactly like a pentachord. To finish the scale, the 3rd finger – the middle finger – swings over and to the right, landing on A. Then it's 2-1, B-C and you're done. Almost.

What goes up must come down.

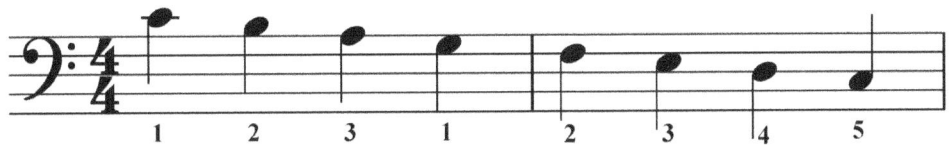

- Play C with your thumb.

- As you play B with your 2nd finger, your hand swivels right and the thumb goes under, moving left.

- Play A with 3 and the thumb continues to pull left.

- Play G with the thumb.

- As your hand straightens out, play F-E-D-C with 2-3-4-5.

Rhythm Gym
Work out with four duration values:

Questions

Q: Why do we have to learn scales? They're boring! And what do we mean by the "key of C?"

A: The words 'key' and 'scale' are tied together in meaning.

When you write or play a melody that uses the notes from the C major scale: C-D-E-F-G-A-B-C, we say you are "in the key of C." If we don't say "major," it's understood that we *mean* major.

A painter has a palette on which he has colors. A musician/composer also has a palette; among the colors on it are scales - groups of note choices. Think of the C scale as a color. And to really learn about that color you have to concentrate on it. One way to do that is to play the scale over and over. Some might find this boring while others find it relaxing - like a meditation. Once the fingering is correct for both hands and automatic, playing a scale can be a peaceful experience.

There are essentially 12 major scales and 12 major keys:

C
C♯ and D♭
D
D♯ and E♭
E
F
F♯ and G♭
G
G♯ and A♭
A
A♯ and B♭
B

We will learn some of these new scales as we progress through the coming chapters. We'll also come to know some of the differences between a key such as F♯ and G♭. For now, let's concentrate on the C major scale.

Guided Practice

Playing one octave of the C scale - up and down, hands together - is today's goal. Earlier in the chapter you played the scale - hands separately. Now it's time to put both hands together. Here's what the music looks like with the fingering.

At first, think of the scale with these moves:

- C-D-E. Both hands. Thumb under R.H. (Right Hand)
- R.H. is now easy 1-2-3-4-5 to finish scale
  L.H. has F-G, 2-1 to complete.
- L.H. 3rd finger now swings over to complete scale.
  A-B-C, 3-2-1, done.
- R.H. going down is 5-4-3-2-1
  L.H. is C-B-A, 1-2-3. Thumb swings left as B(2) is played.
- L.H. thumb is now on G, 1
  L.H. completes with F-E-D-C, 2-3-4-5
- When R.H. thumb gets to F, 3 comes over to complete E-D-C, 3-2-1

The good news is once you've learned this fingering, it can be used for other particular scales.

Now that you've learned 8 notes in each hand, spend some time reinforcing those notes reading music on the following pages.

Music for Sight Reading and Practice

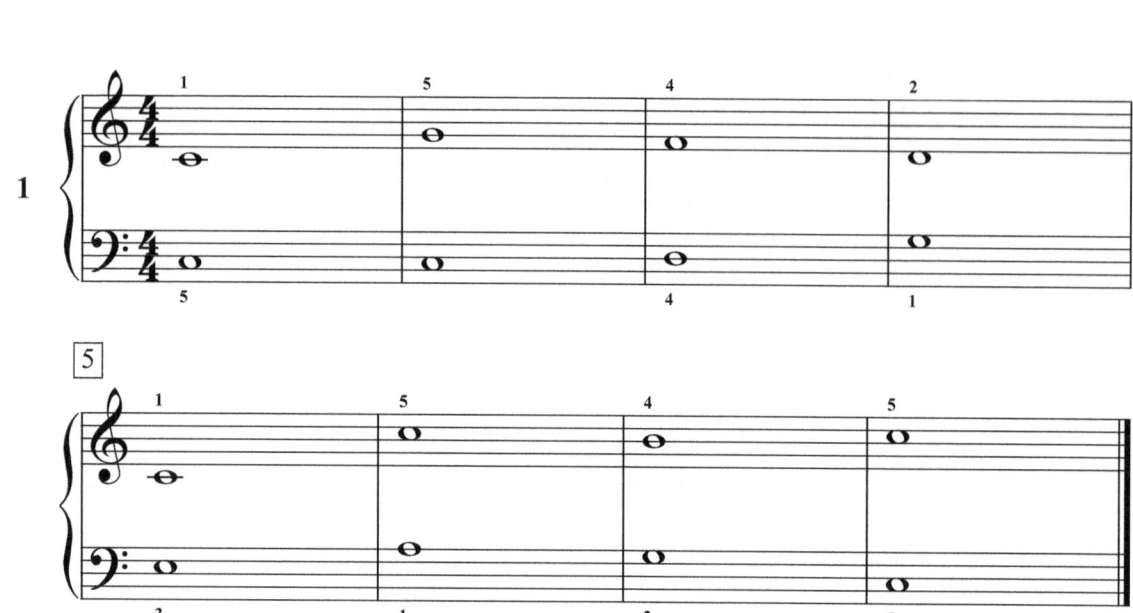

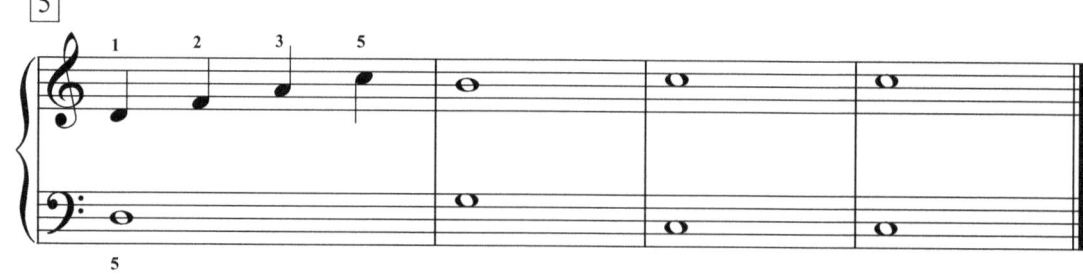

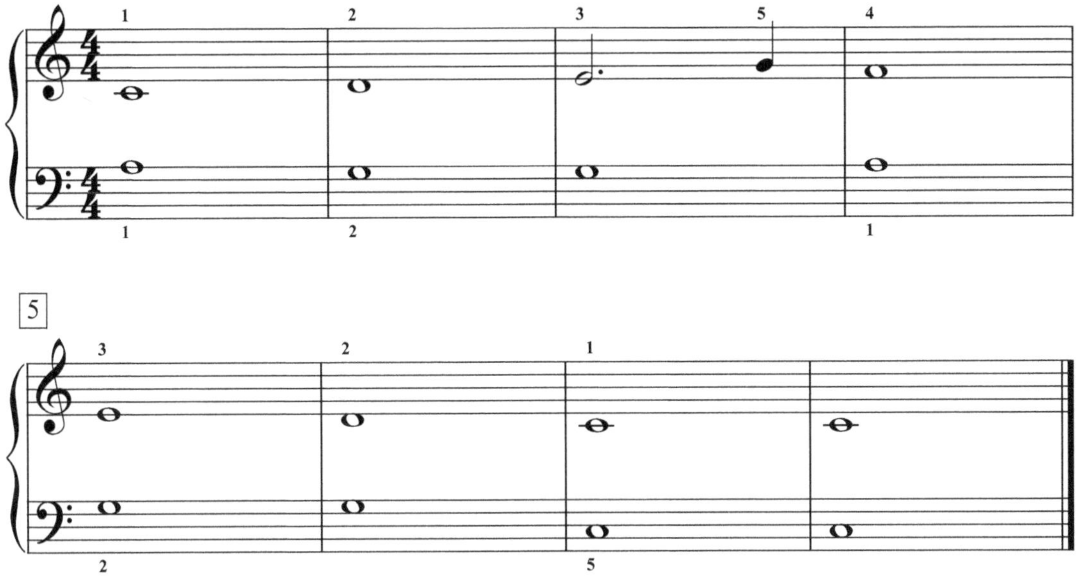

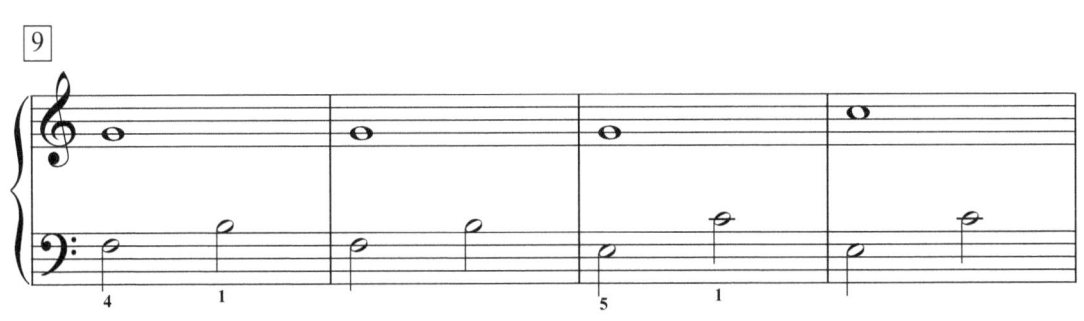

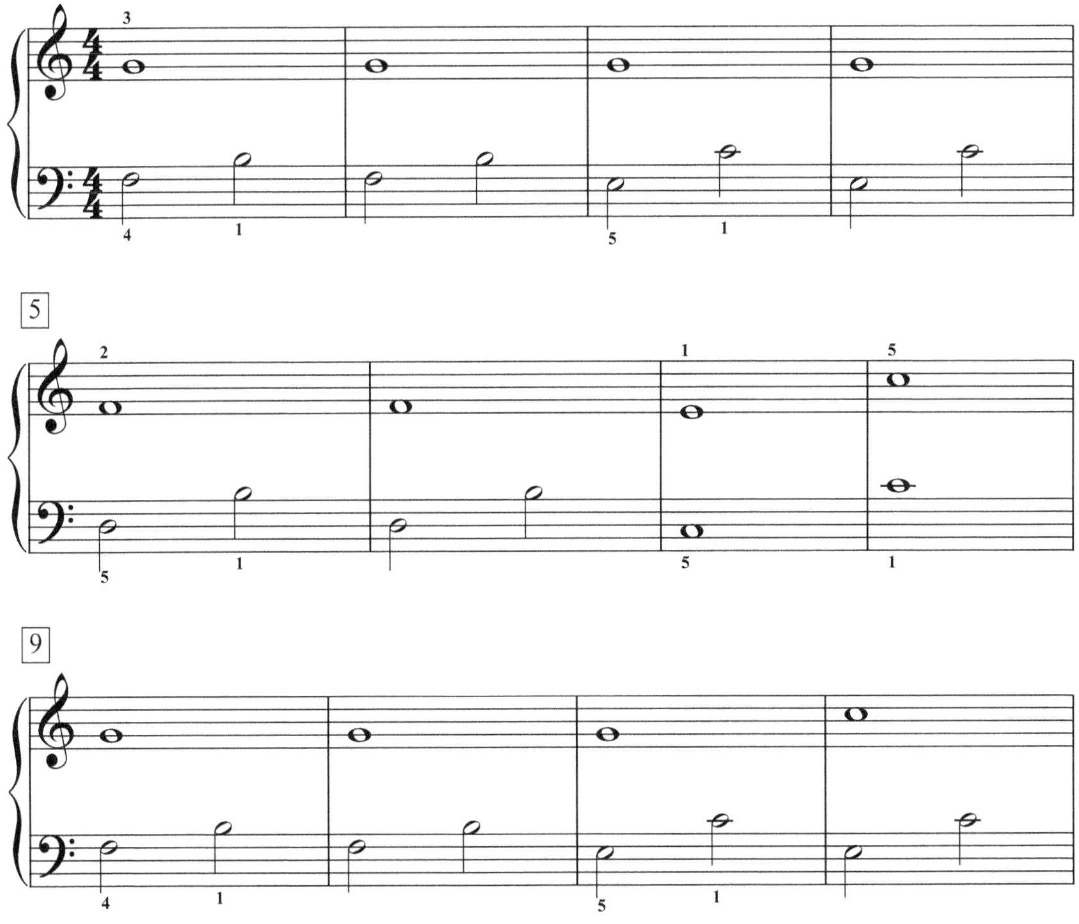

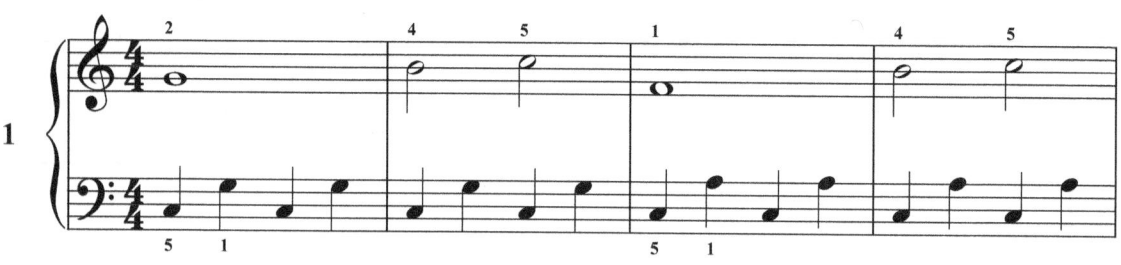

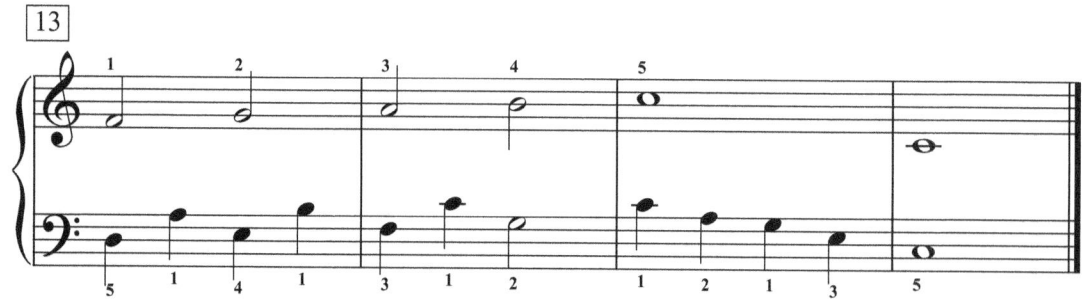

Chipping Away

CHAPTER THREE

Memory Check

These are the 16 notes you need to know before going on.

The good news is that if you know these notes, you're halfway to your goal of 30 notes or 4 octaves. If you need more work on recognizing and playing these first two octaves, use your flash cards or go back to the previous exercises.

New Notes: Treble Clef

Today we continue to go higher in pitch from where we left off at C above middle C. The new notes are D-E-F-G-A. They look like this:

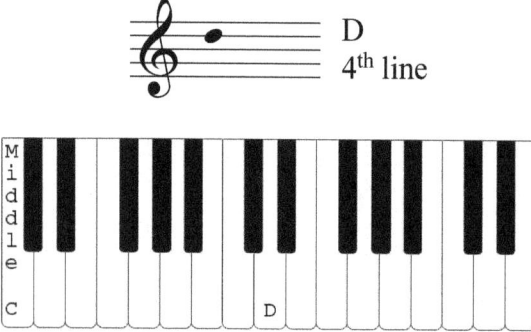

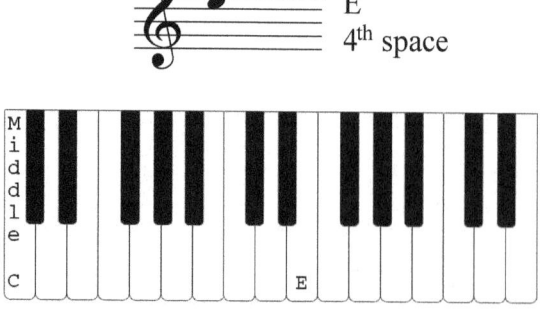

To the right of C,
in the middle of Black Group 2

To the left of F,
to the right of Black Group 2

To the right of E,
to the left of Black Group 3

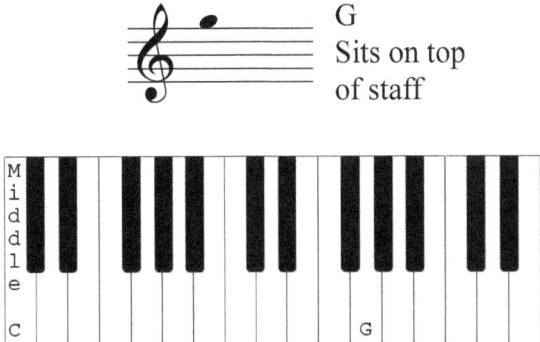

To the right of F,
to the left of A

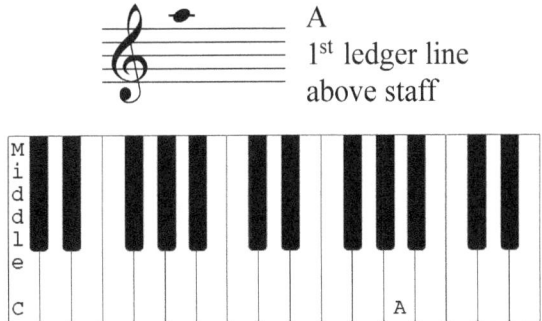

To the right of G,
to the left of B

1

2

Twinkle, Twinkle

Echo In The Bathroom

Free Pizza

Free Pizza With Toppings

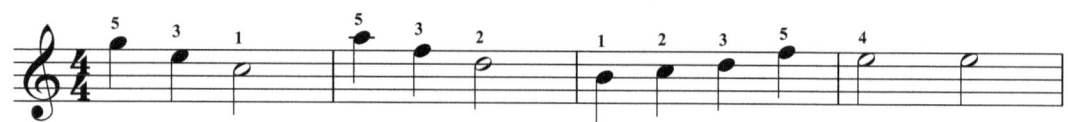

iPods, iPods

Bingo, The Gambling Dog

What The Heck?

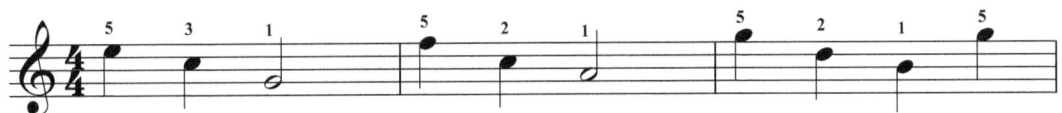

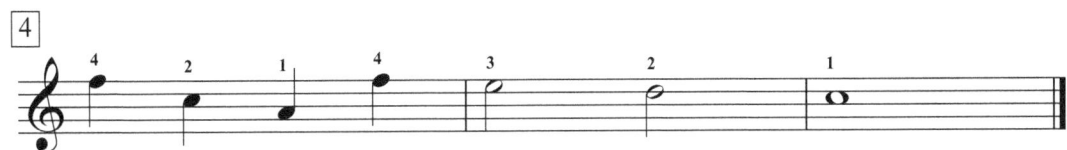

Where Did Fido Go?

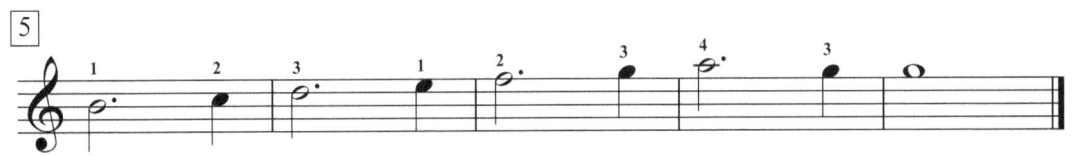

Waiting For Finals

New Notes: Bass Clef
Continuing down after C below middle C are B-A-G-F-E:

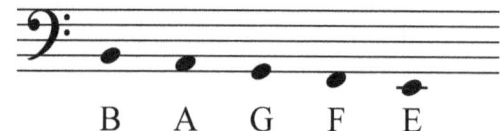

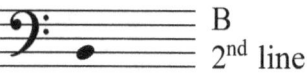

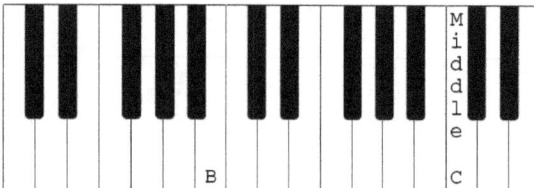

To the left of C,
to the right of Black Group 3

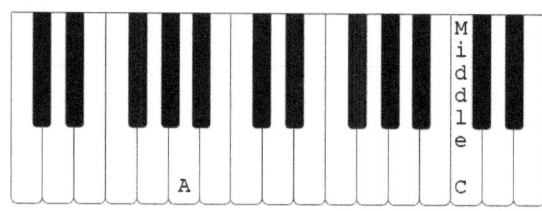

To the right of G,
to the left of B

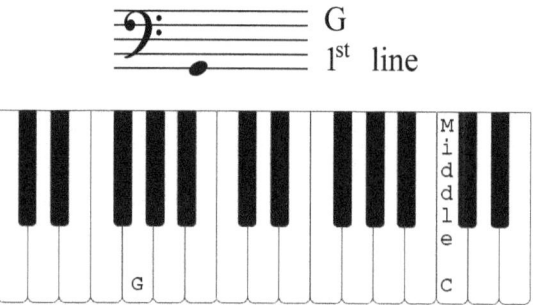

To the right of F,
to the left of A

To the right of E,
to the left of Black Group 3

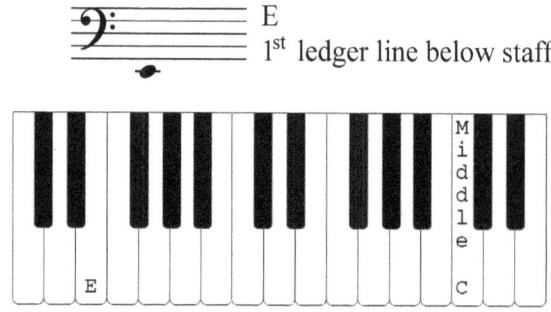

To the left of F,
to the right of Black Group 2

Getting There

Something Spanish

Prepare To Surf

Hit The Road, Toad

Haunted

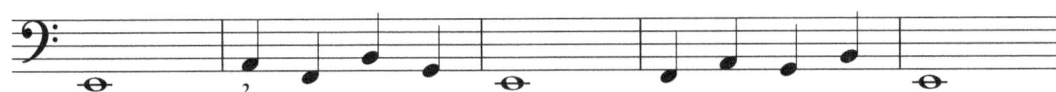

Just For Laughs

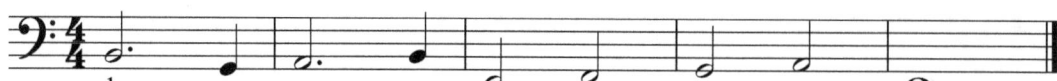

Everybody Gets A Present

Muddy

Yearning For The Motherland

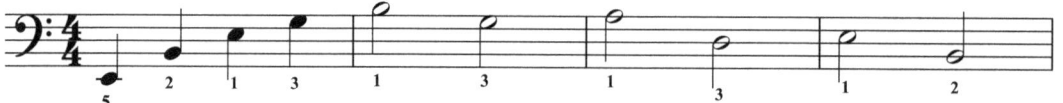

Disco Preparedness

The Power Of Simplicity

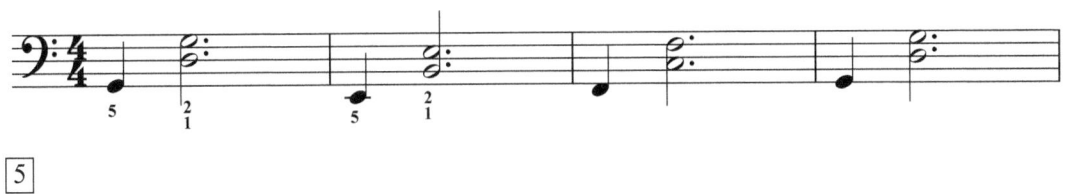

Ghost Town

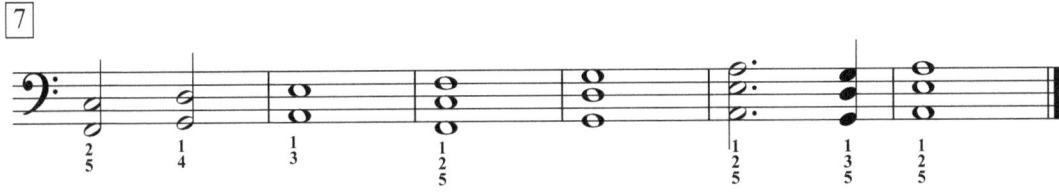

Nightline On Elm Street

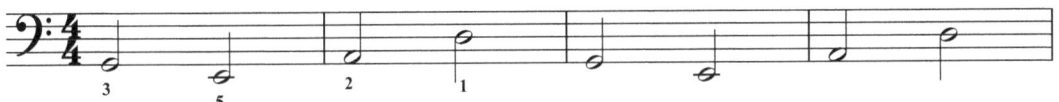
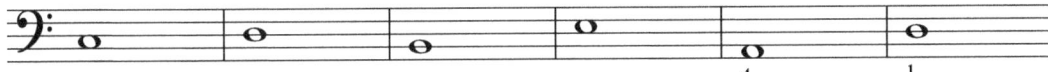

Zombie Karaoke

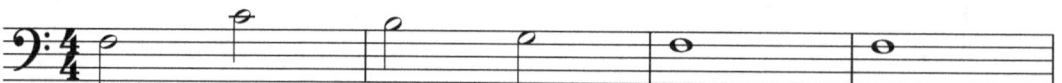

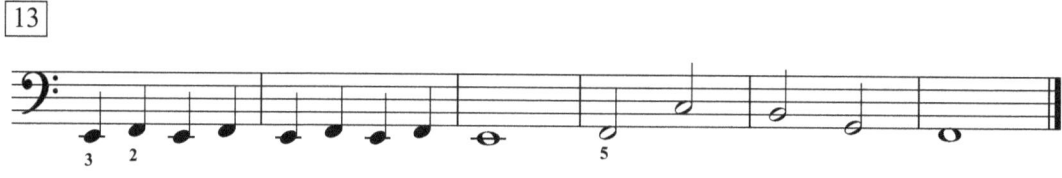

The Littlest Walter

Chromatic

It's time to have a deeper discussion of the black keys of the piano. We said in Chapter One that context gives meaning to the black keys. Here's what we mean. If you are working your way up, the chromatic notes are called SHARPS. This is the sharp symbol ♯ and you place it to the left of the actual note.

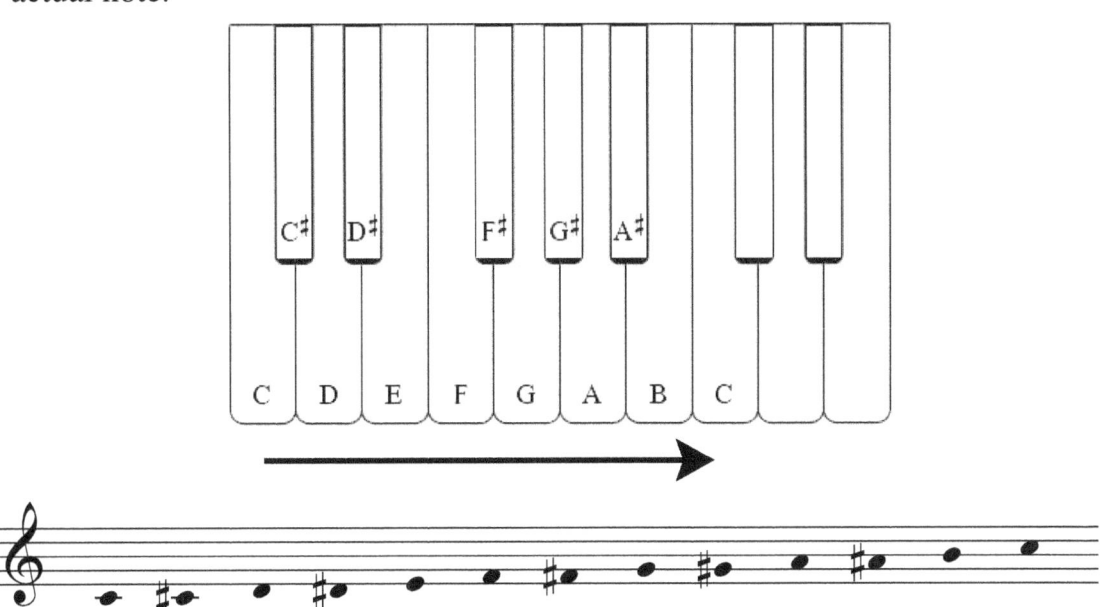

If you are working your way down, the chromatic notes are called FLATS. You put this symbol ♭ to the left of the note.

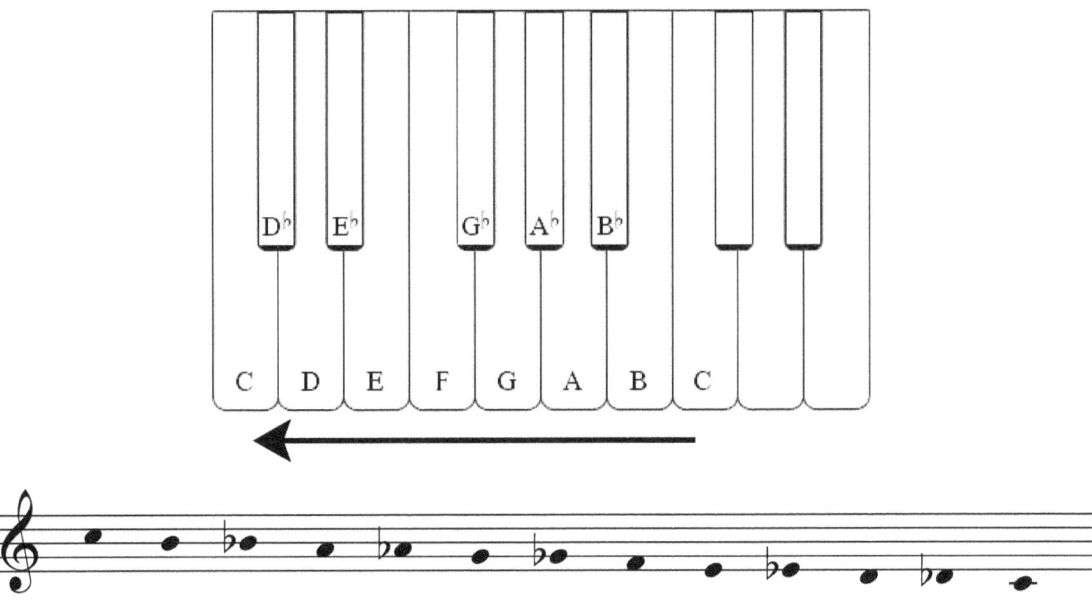

63

Typical pieces of music should look like this:

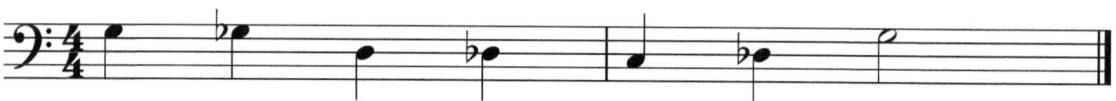

If you start, arbitrarily, on Middle C and go up like this

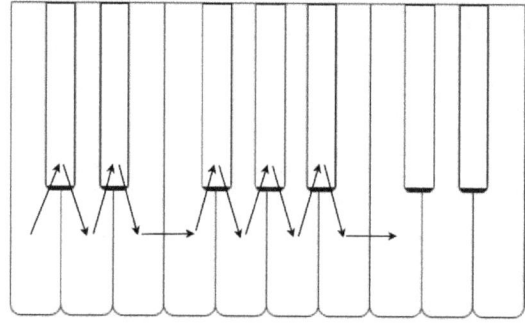

or, from the octave above Middle C, go down like this

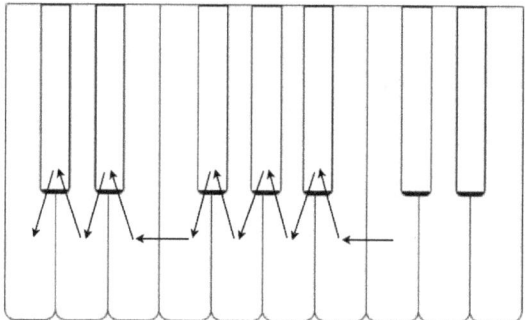

you've just played a 12 note CHROMATIC SCALE. You've used every note between Middle C and the next higher C. If you wrote or played a melody that used many or all of these 12 notes, we'd say, "The melody was CHROMATIC."

One of the most famous chromatic melodies is Flight of the Bumble Bee. When written out in quarter notes, the first phrase looks like this.

If you were using only the 7 notes of the C scale or another 7-note scale, we'd say, "The melody is DIATONIC." If a few sharps or flats were mixed in with the naturally occurring 7 notes of that scale, we'd say, "The melody contains a little chromaticism." Flight of the Bumble Bee is very chomatic.

In addition to the sharp ♯ and flat ♭ symbols, we have something called the NATURAL ♮ . What the natural does is negate the sharp or flat within the measure that it appears. It also serves as a reminder in the next bar(♮) not to sharp or flat a note anymore.

New Scale: G

Now that you're completely familiar with the sharps and flats of the piano, it's time to learn some new major scales containing sharps or flats.

If we start on the note G above middle C and apply the formula for a major scale

```
W   W   H   W   W   W   H
1   1  1/2  1   1   1  1/2
```

here's what we get:

Because this scale contains an F sharp, it would be tedious to have to write that F♯ over and over when we needed it in a melody. So, we put that F♯ at the beginning of our piece of music that is in the key of G. It looks like this

and is called a KEY SIGNATURE.

Now we can write music like this

and all the F's will get sharped automatically because of the key signature.

When a musician looks at a piece of music for the first time, he or she checks out the key signature and the time signature. This is a habit you *must* get into. Many note mistakes come from *not* looking at the key signature. Don't let it happen to you!

Good news: The fingering for the scale of G is *exactly* like the fingering for the scale of C.

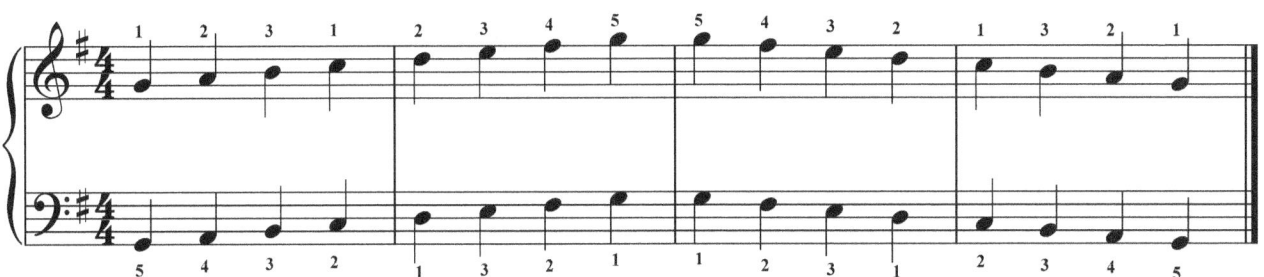

Read and practice the following exercises and pieces.

67

Two Notes At Once

1

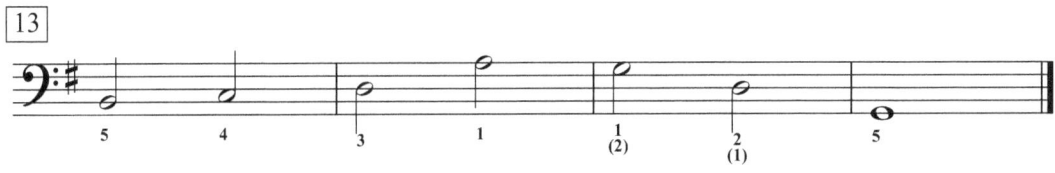

2

3

1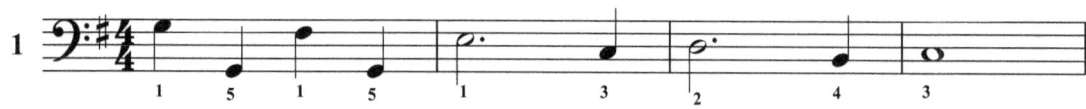

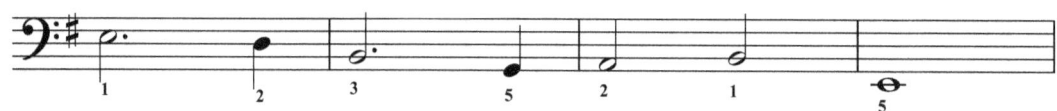

2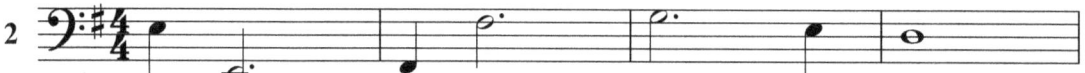
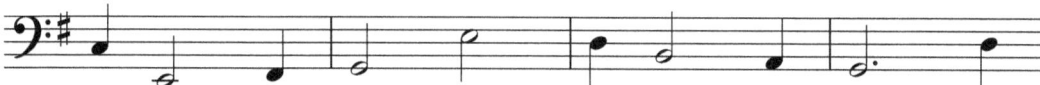
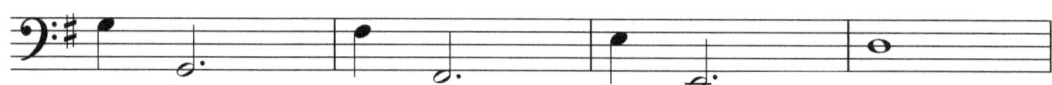

Somewhere Far From Here

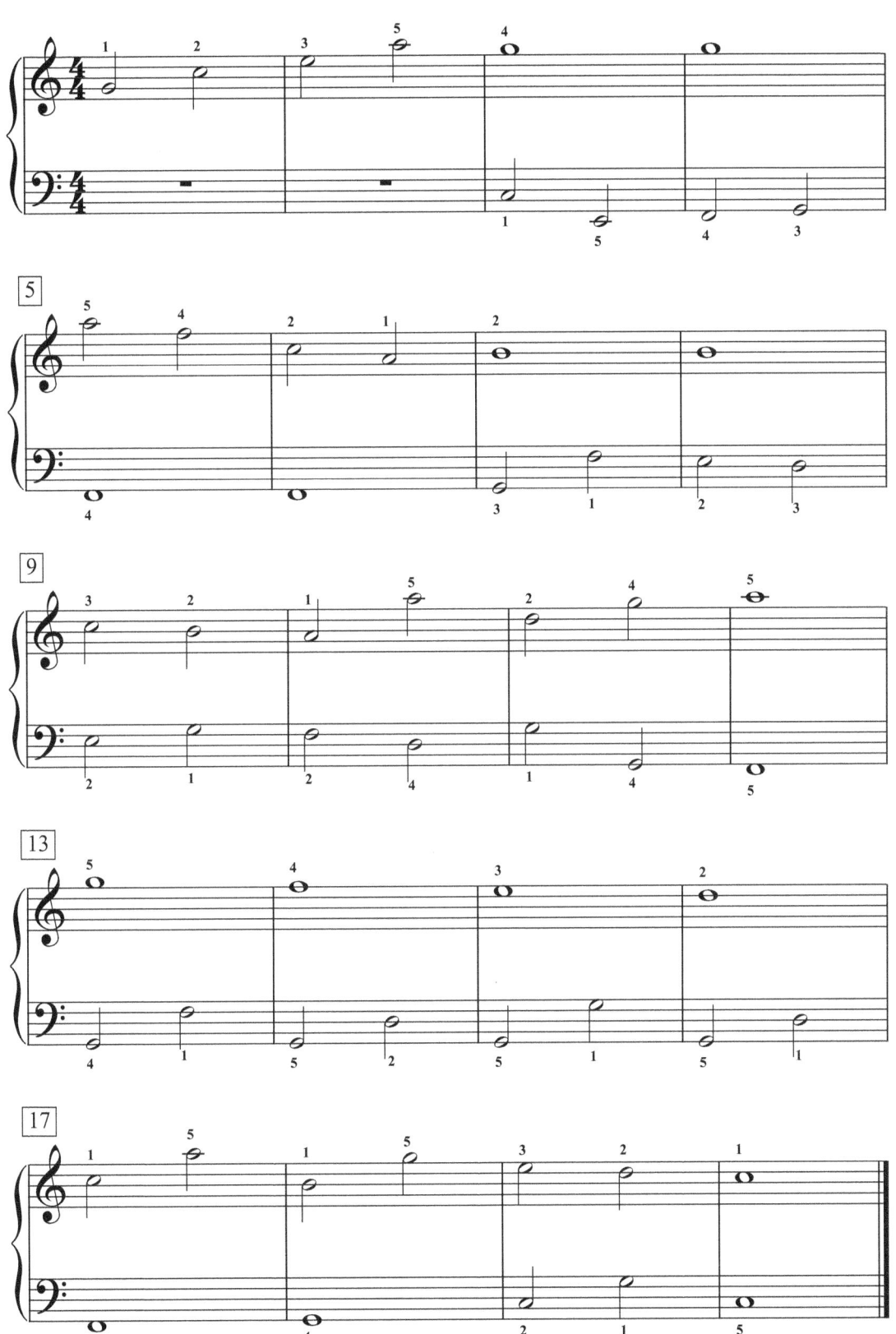

Taco Bell's Taco

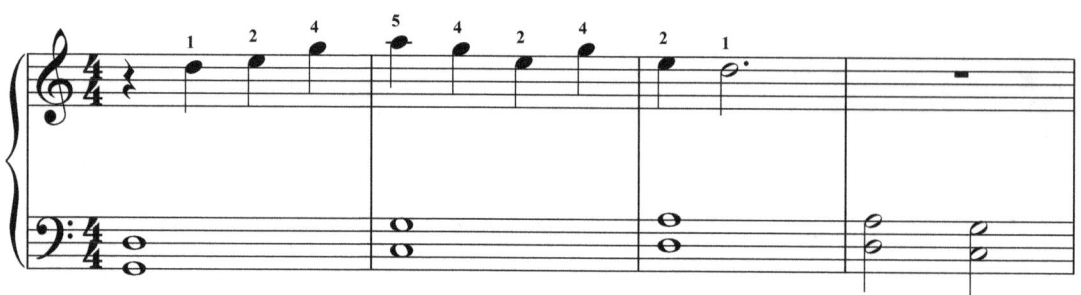

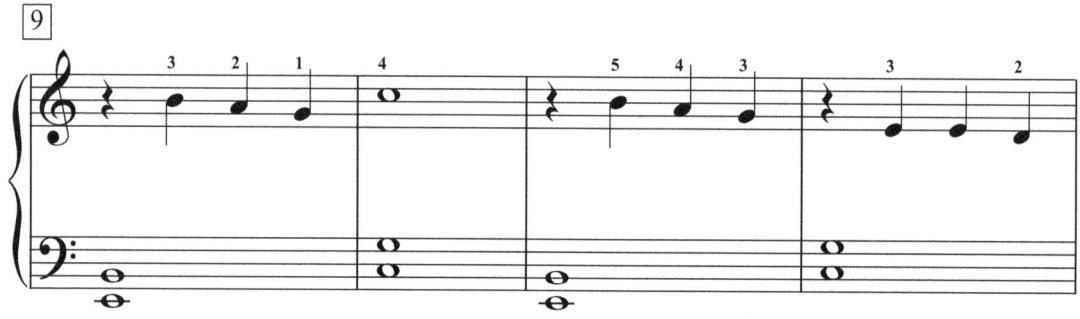

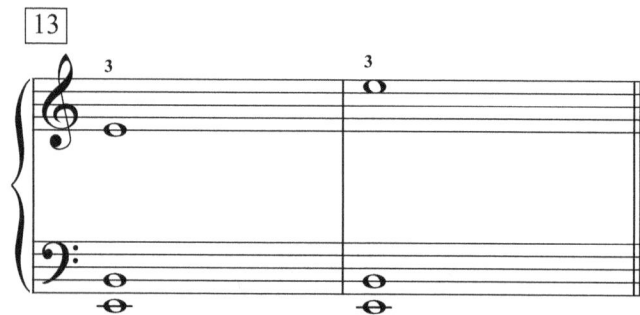

Pachelbel's Canon - Whole Note Version

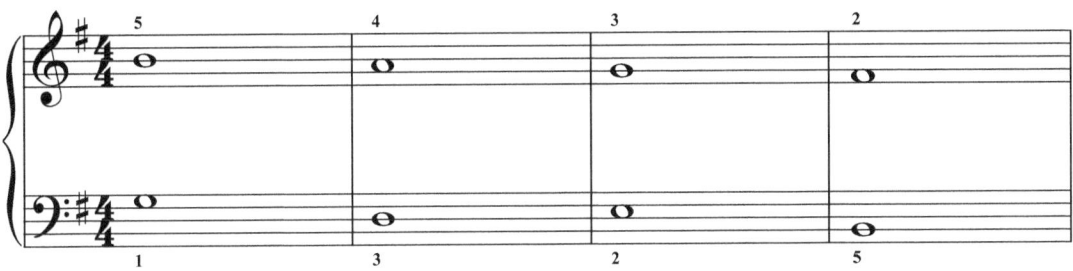
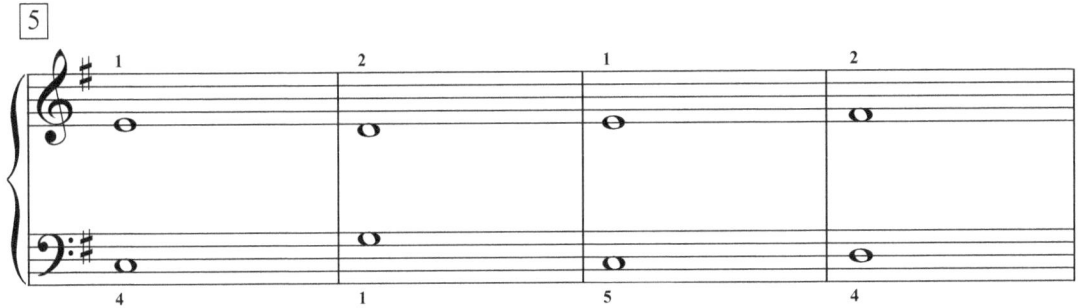
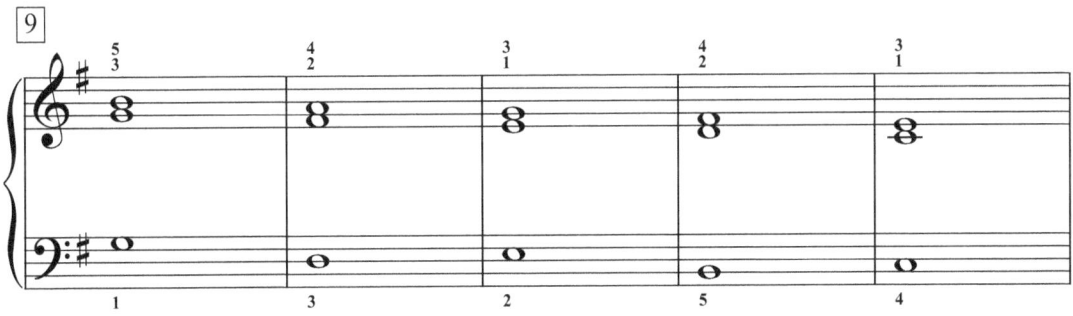
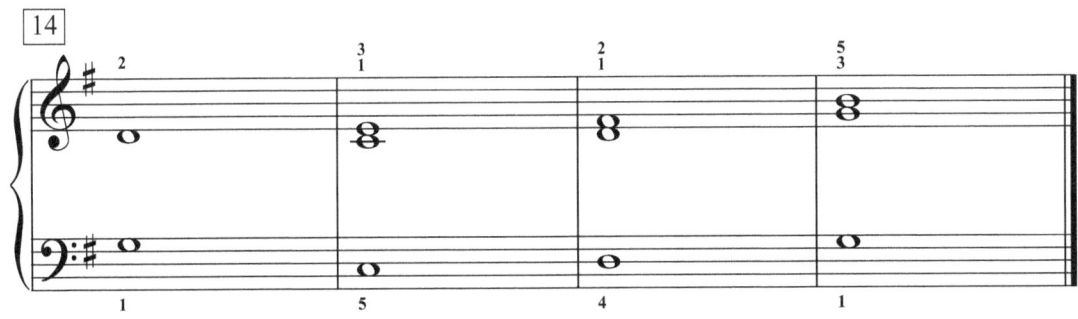

New Scale: F

When you apply the formula for a major scale starting on F, here is what you get:

Since there is a B♭ in the scale, we put it in the key signature. Now the scale looks like this:

Sadly, the fingering in the right hand is different from C and G. Here's how it's done.

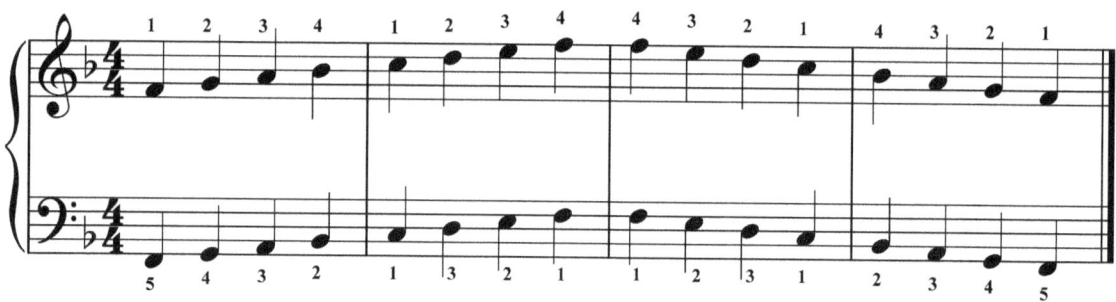

Practice the following exercises and pieces in the key of F.

Every Day With You

Stem Direction

When you break a quarter note into its simplest parts you get a note head and a stem . Put together, it looks like this ♩ or this ♩.

The idea behind stem direction is to have as much of the note head and stem as possible on the staff so it's easier for the eye to take in. Based on the notes we've studied so far, here is what determines stem direction:

In treble clef, from Middle C to A, *stems go up*.
From B above middle C upward and beyond, *stems go down*.

In bass clef, from E to C, *stems go up*.
From D upwards to Middle C and beyond, *stems go down*.

Here are some examples of the stem direction principle at work.

Definitions & Symbols: Ties, Rests and Repeat Signs

So far we've used these duration symbols:

♩ = 1 Beat

𝅗𝅥 = 2 Beats

𝅗𝅥. = 3 Beats

𝅝 = 4 Beats

What if we want a note that lasts 5 beats? A dotted whole note gives 6 beats so we need a new symbol. That symbol is called the TIE, looks like this and equals the value of the note plus the note it is attached to (tied to).

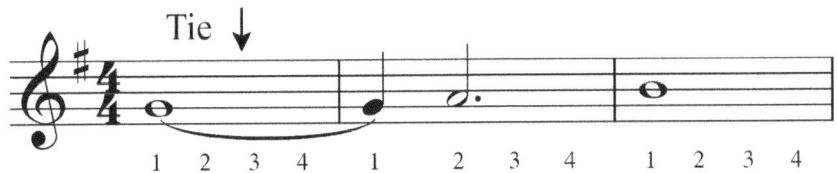

The whole note *tied* to the quarter note is held for 5 beats (4 + 1).

In the following example the 4th beat of bar 1 is tied to the first beat of bar 2. The whole idea is *you don't play the F of bar 2. You hold it, you feel the pulse go by, but you <u>don't</u> repeat it.*

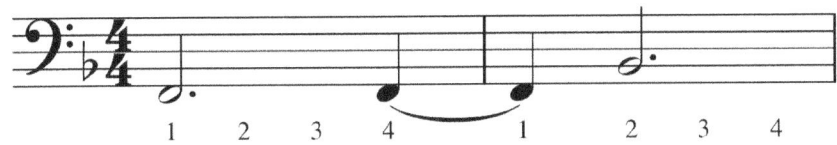

Another situation that comes up in music is the portrayal of silence. How do we notate silence, nothing, silencio, nada? The symbols for silence are called RESTS. They look like this in comparison to the note durations they represent:

Note	Rest Equivalent	Rest Name
♩	𝄽	Quarter rest
♪ (half)	𝄼	Half rest
dotted half note	𝄼 • *	Dotted half rest
𝅝	𝄻	Whole rest

Notice below that the half rest *sits on top of the 3rd line* whereas the whole rest *hangs off the 4th line*.

Here's how rests look when incorporated into music. Since they are indicating silence, remember to take your hand off the keys when they appear but keep the 1-2-3-4 count cycling.

Another symbol that's very useful is the REPEAT SIGN. Rather than rewrite 4 or 8 or 16 bars of music that you want to repeat exactly (time consuming), all you have to do is write this:

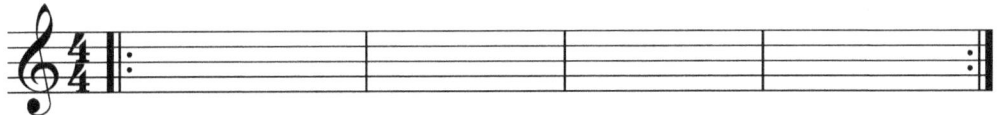

These symbols tell the player to repeat exactly what he or she just played. If the composer wants it repeated more than once, they write this:

Anacrusis

Not all music starts on beat 1. If a composer wants the music to begin on beat 4, for example

we call this an ANACRUSIS. It is also know as an UPBEAT or a PICKUP. The definition of DOWNBEAT is beat 1. Any musical phrase that begins on anything other than the downbeat is said to be a pickup, anacrusis, or upbeat.

A New Time Signature: 3/4

Another time signature that is used frequently is 3/4.

- Three beats to the measure

- A quarter note gets one beat

3/4 time is probably most famously used in the waltz.

Blue Danube Waltz
Johann Strauss

Skater's Waltz
Emil Waldteufel

Baby Falls From Tree, Film At Eleven

Fake Medieval

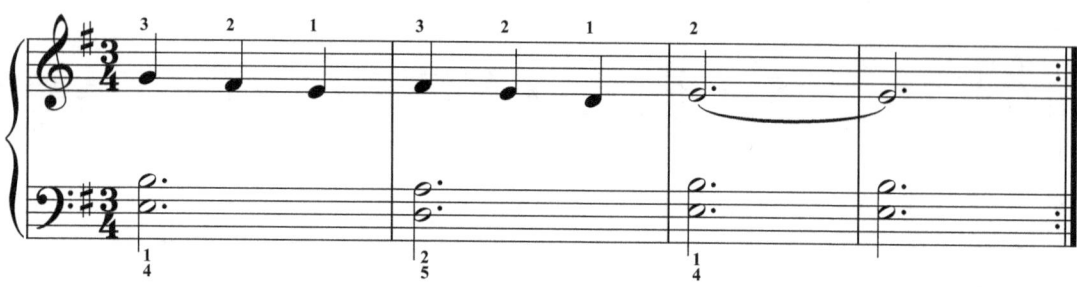

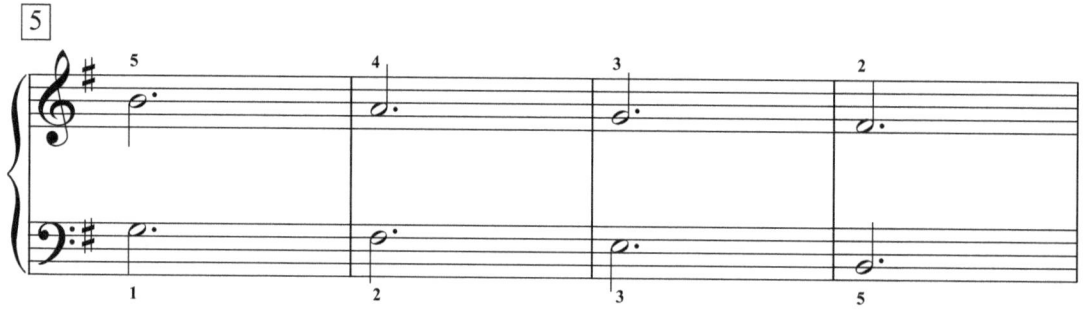

* The whole rest symbol means exactly what it says - rest for the 'whole' bar. In 4/4 time it stands for 4 beats; in 3/4 time it stands for the whole bar or 3 beats.

Bluebird Pie

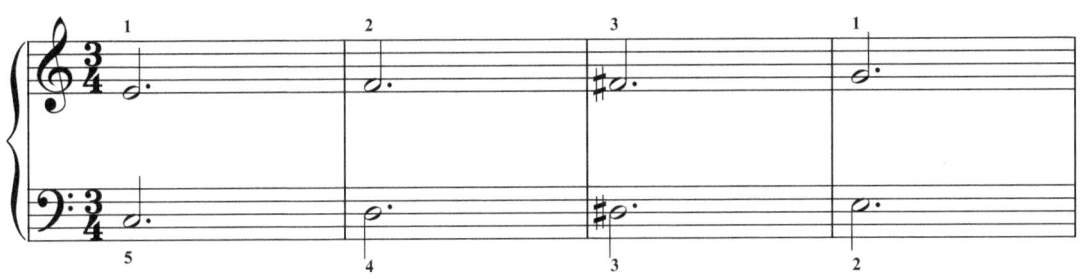
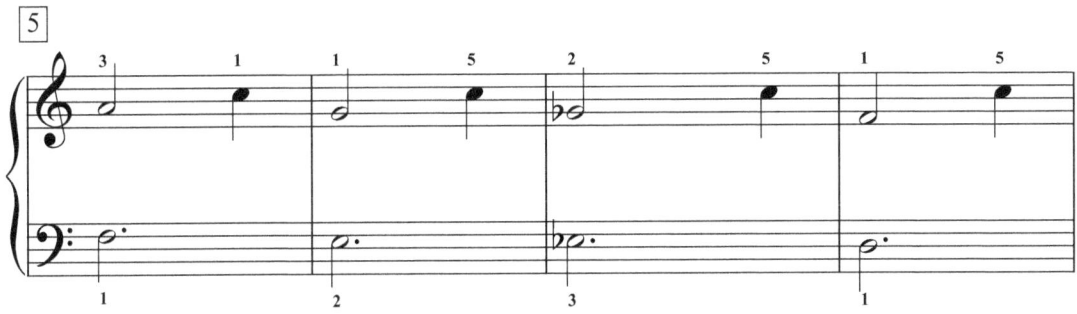
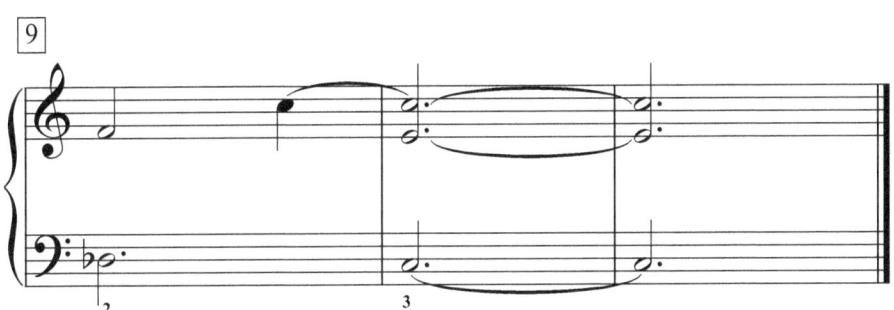

Switzerland, Land Of Chocolate

Belgium, Land Of More Chocolate

New Intervals: Minor and Major Thirds

The next intervals to be studied are the THIRDS (3rds).

A minor 3rd, written m3, consists of a step and a half, a whole tone and a half tone.

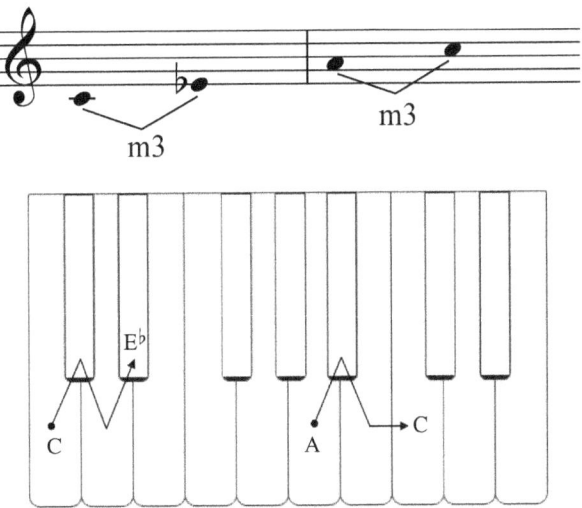

A major 3rd, written M3, consists of 2 steps, 2 whole tones.

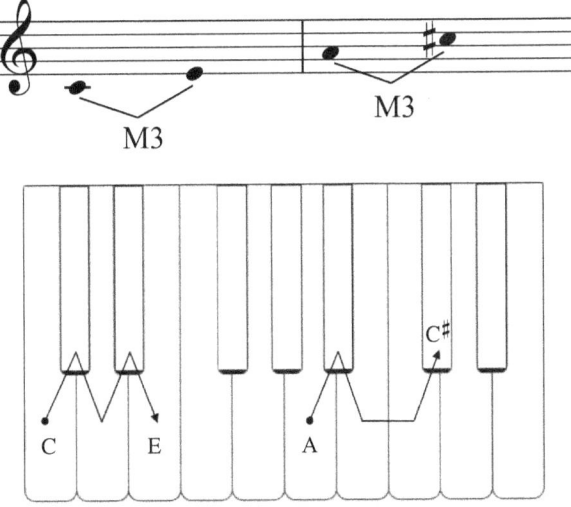

Why Study Chords?

Chords are the simplest and most modern way of writing out popular music. Most classical music indicates every note. Popular music - written in chord-melody style also known as a 'lead sheet' - is a simple and elegant way to communicate a lot of information to the player who then exercises their creativity as they interpret what they see. Memorizing chords gives you the ability to play any piece of popular music written in this way.

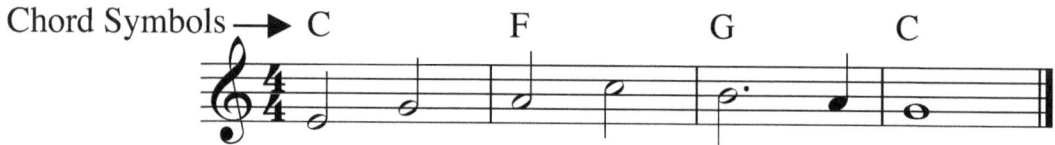

Where Do Chords Come From?

The simplest chords – also known as TRIADS – come from scales. If we write out the C major scale

and then, observing the key signature (in this case - no sharps or flats) stack a 3rd and then another 3rd on the notes of the scale, we get 7 chords.

When we analyze the 1st, 4th, and 5th chord, we see that they're constructed in exactly the same way. We call them MAJOR CHORDS. These three chords are also known as the PRIMARY CHORDS or the PRIMARY TRIADS.

Formula for a major chord = major third on the bottom, and a minor third on top.

We name these chords after the scale degree or note name they're based on.

And just like the scale, all we have to say is C or F or G to imply major. For example, you'd say, "Play a C, F and G" not "C major, F major and G major."

In music theory we have logical names and designations for these three chords.

The One Chord	The Four Chord	The Five Chord
The Tonic	The Subdominant	The Dominant
I	IV	V
1	4	5

All of these terms or numbering systems refer to the FUNCTION of the chord. For now, think of the chord's function as its job.

The TONIC is usually where a piece of music starts. It anchors the music and gives it a point of reference.

The DOMINANT, as its name implies, is the next strongest chord. Essentially, the dominant brings you back to the tonic. I to V and back to I is one of the simplest progressions there is. A PROGRESSION is a series of chords. Many simple songs are based on this two chord progression: Polly Wolly Doodle, Row Row Row Your Boat, Three Blind Mice, The Farmer in the Dell, Pop Goes the Weasel, Eensy Weensy Spider.

The next simplest progressions bring in the SUBDOMINANT chord. I-IV-V-I or I-IV-I-V-I are good examples. Folk songs such as 'La Bamba' and early rock and roll such as 'Twist and Shout' are based on the I-IV-V-I progression. Many of Bob Dylan's early songs use only these three chords.

Once you've memorized the notes of the C, F, and G chords there are thousands of songs using the I-IV-V progression that you can play…but only in the key of C.

Previously we stated there are 12 major keys. The reasons we would want to play a song or piece of music in a key other than C are many.

Tessitura and Transposition, Part I

Every voice and every instrument has a group of notes where it sounds the strongest. That is called the TESSITURA.

Here is the tessitura of Jessica. Her voice, for a girl, is a little low. We call that an alto. Many altos can sing the G below middle C, but not Jessica.

Compare that to the tessitura of Noriko, a soprano, whose voice is higher in pitch.

Middle C, D or E sounds weak when Noriko sings it. So if the range of a song is an octave from tonic to octave using C to C as an example, Noriko would have to sing the same song in the key of F. And the pianist accompanying Noriko would have to transpose.

TRANSPOSE means to look at a piece of music in one key, and play it in another. In this case: look at the music in C and play it in F. Here's where knowing chords and functions is useful.

If you know that the chords of a song are C, F and G, you also know the progression is I-IV-V. To play that same song higher, in the key of F – Noriko's key – here's what you do:

1. Write out or think out the scale of F

2. Fill in the 3rds to the 1st 5 notes of the scale

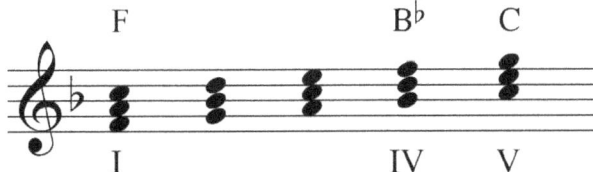

3. Play the song in F using the new chords

Once you've memorized the I, IV and V chords in many keys, you can skip step 2.

Let's say that putting the song in F is good for Noriko but her friend, Jennifer, wants to sing it and needs the key to be G. No problem – you figure out the I, IV, and V chord in the new key.

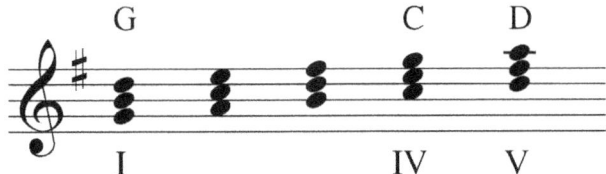

To recap, here are the I, IV and V chords to 3 keys.

Key of C: C F G

Key of F: F B♭ C

Key of G: G C D

You can see that there are some duplications. If you memorize 5 chords: C, F, G, D and B♭ you can play many simple songs in 3 keys!

Given the notes you know so far, and also what combinations of notes sound good, here are the left hand voicings you'll need to play the pieces at the end of this chapter. VOICINGS are simply the notes of a chord in a particular order. For example: The chord of F can be voiced F-A-C or A-C-F or C-F-A.

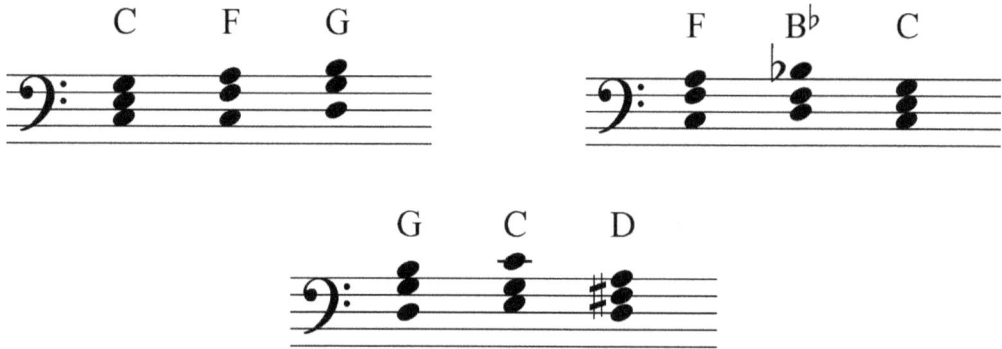

The most popular way to interpret a chord chart is to play the chord with the right hand. In your left hand (for now) play the note that the chord is named after - an octave lower. The simplest approach would be to play a whole or half note for every chord you see.

The simplest way to use chords is by placing them in a CHART. A chord chart is exactly like it sounds; a representation of music via its chords. Here are some examples.

Simple Chord Chart

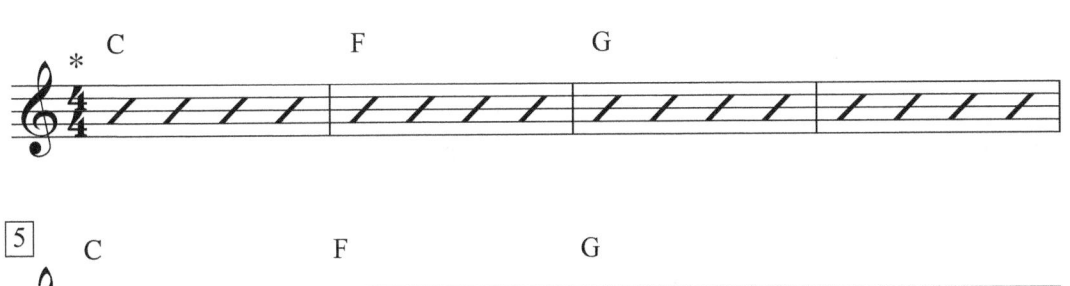

Another Simple Chord Chart

*The slash marks help you keep your place or keep count.

Nashville Number System

Besides the tonic, subdominant, and dominant Roman numeral I IV V designations, there is another system that is equally effective and useful called the Nashville Number System.

For the three chords in question, it is simply 1   4   5.

The most common use of this system is in country music. Like the Roman numerals it is equally elegant and to the point. All a player has to do is learn the numbers and the corresponding chords in every key and transposition is instantaneous. It's actually much easier than transposing chord symbols, but chords are more efficient and straightforward when music gets complex.

Here is the chord chart in C you just saw, rewritten in the Nashville Number System.

```
C:   1   4   5   5
     1   4   5   5
     4   5   1   1
     4   5   1   1
```

For brevity's sake, musicians may communicate these chords to each other like this, "The first part is fourteen fifty five twice, then forty five eleven twice."

Blue Moon of Kentucky

```
1   4   1     5
1   4   1/5*  1
4   1   4     1/5
1   4   1/5   1
```

*This is called a 'split bar:' Two beats on the 1 chord, two beats on the 5 chord.

94

Rhythm Gym

Since we have added ties and rests to our knowledge of duration symbols, let's use them to get better at sightreading. Get the pulse of either 4 or 3 in your head, pick a doable tempo, and go for it!

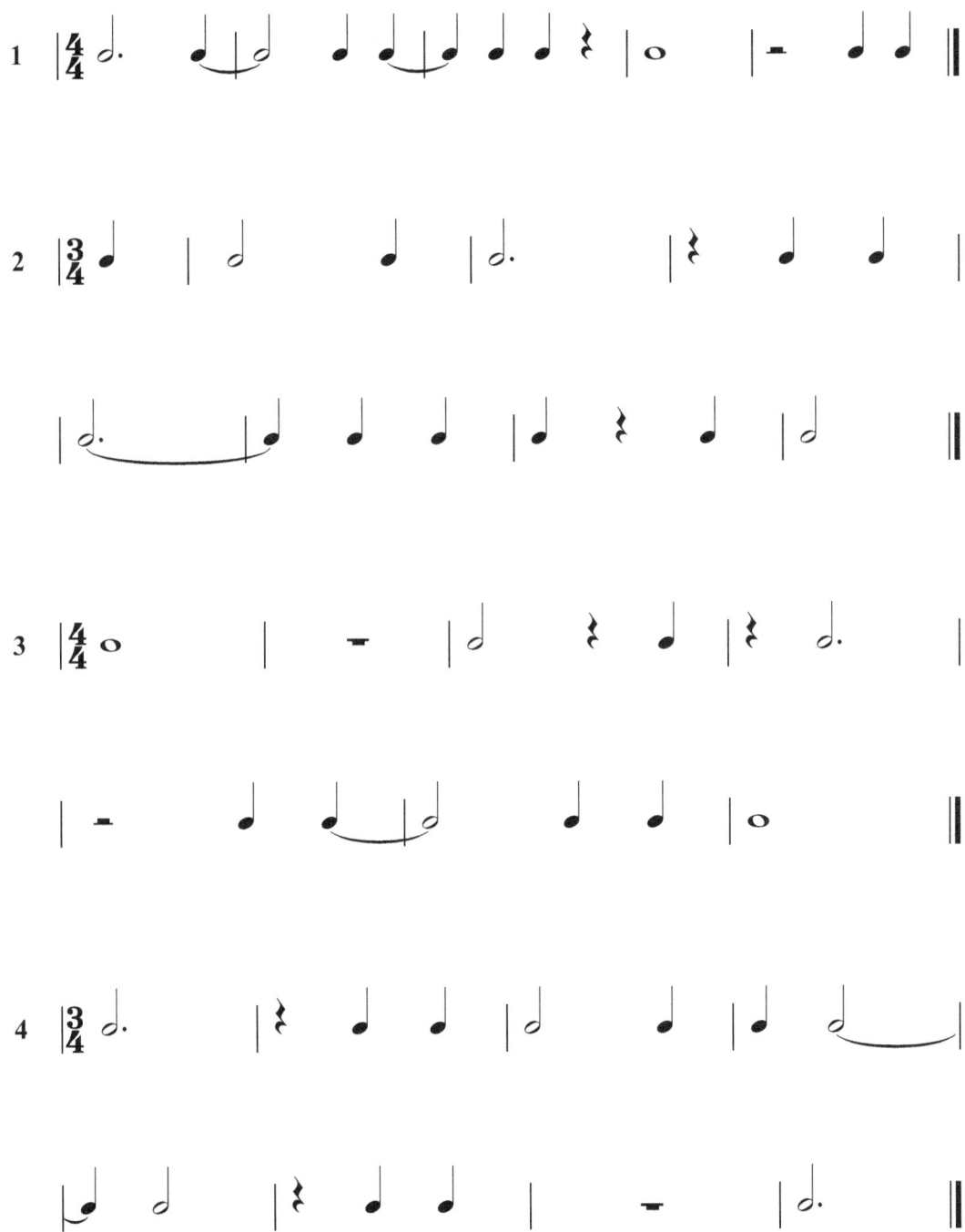

*Generally, a bar of 4/4 should easily divide into 2 beats + 2 beats but ♩♩‿♩♩ is more easily read as ♩ ♩ ♩ and has been accepted as a better, simpler figure for hundreds of years.

Questions

Q: I loved the key of C because I never made a mistake. Now with these new keys of F with B♭ and G with F♯ I'm making mistakes all over the place. What can I do?

A: Unless you are planning to spend a lifetime playing only on the white keys of the piano, you have to memorize key signatures and be able to apply that knowledge to your playing. That's one of the positive outcomes of learning scales; the other is fingering.

Before you play a piece of music, look at the time signature and get that in your head and decide at what tempo you're going to play. Then, look at the key signature and get those sharps or flats in your head. There are lots of things to eventually watch out for when reading a piece of music. Knowing the sharps or flats perfectly is like having a security blanket. Ultimately you should FEAR NO KEY!

Q: Is learning to transpose really necessary? Can't I just skip it?
A: You can skip it, but you will limit your work possibilities.

One of the things most pianists or accompanists are called on to do is to transpose. If you can't transpose, you will work less, and live in fear of being asked to do so. If you're writing a song and it's too high for your voice, you'll need to transpose it lower so you can sing it. If you've written a piece of music for an instrument - let's say a trumpet - and they can't play it in the key you wrote it in, it's nice to be able to say, "Let's put that in a better key for you," rather than make them play it in the difficult, unplayable original key. Knowing how to transpose makes you a more complete musician.

Guided Practice: Principles of Fingering

Fingering. What's it all about? How do you do it? How do you figure out what's a good fingering, and how do you avoid bad fingerings?

The answer to all these questions is to *look ahead, anticipate, and remember that your hands are not glued to the keyboard - they can go anywhere.*

When you look at the left hand of this new piece by Bach, you can see that the span or range of notes is normal - low E to G. The five fingers of the left hand can easily cover these notes. Play through this left hand part using the suggested fingering.

The first two bars of the right hand span five notes. G is the bottom note and D is the top note so it makes sense to put 3 on the first note of B.

The next fingering decision comes on the first note of bar three. If you use 4 again for the second C, you'll run out of fingers, start overusing 4 and 5, and your hand will look like a crab scurrying sideways. The solution to bar three and beyond is to *pick your hand up and pull your thumb right* until it is in position to play the C. Then the hand moves slightly right and plays E with 3.

Bar five is played with 5, 3, 2 because you have to reserve your thumb for the G of bar six.

Bars six, seven, and eight are good examples of why we learn certain fingerings for certain scales. Can you see that the notes of these bars are members of the G scale? All you're doing is going up and down following the G scale fingering. Even at bar ten, putting 3 on F♯ is the natural finger to descend the G scale.

What to do at bar eleven has to do with the top note of the phrase which is the C of D-F♯-A-C. The hand naturally wants to finger D-F♯-A as 1-3-5 but because of the C you have to reserve the 5th finger and play the notes with 1-2-3-5.

At bar twelve, why not play 5-4-3? Because *the 4th finger is the weakest finger*. Therefore, 5-3-2 puts you in a better position to play bars thirteen and fourteen.

And why at bar eighteen are we using 1-3-4 instead of the more natural 1-2-3? Because of the stretch that has to be made down to the E with the thumb in bar nineteen.

At bar 21 swivel the hand to accommodate 2 on D, then swivel back to place 5 on G.

Jesu, Joy of Man's Desiring

J.S. Bach

Music for Sight Reading and Practice

Primary Triads In C

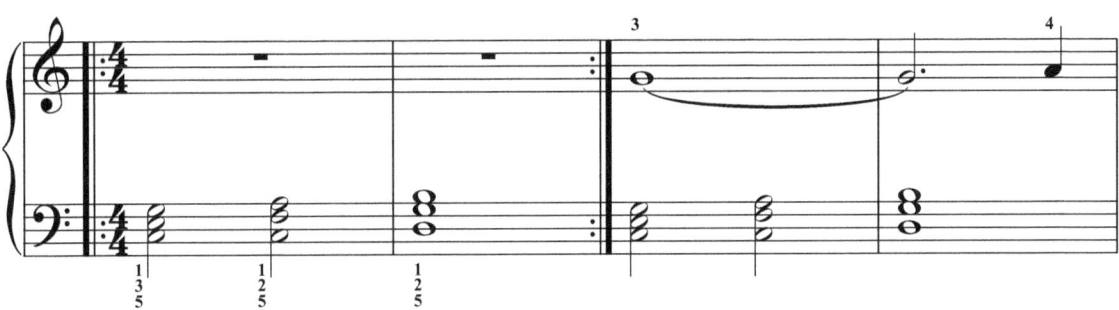
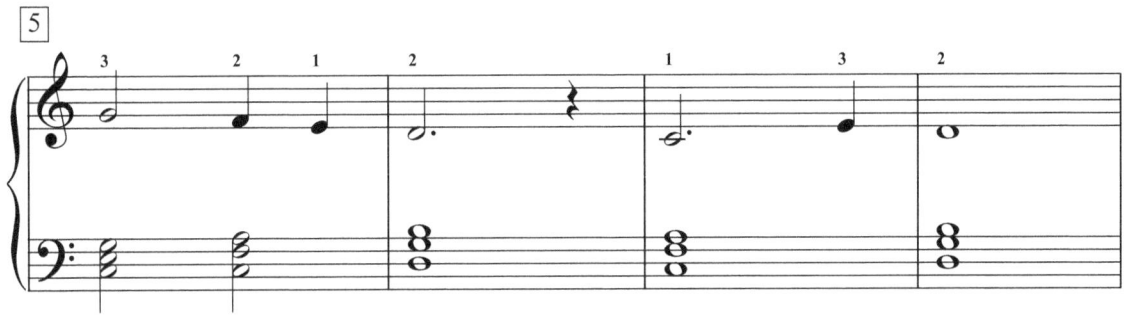
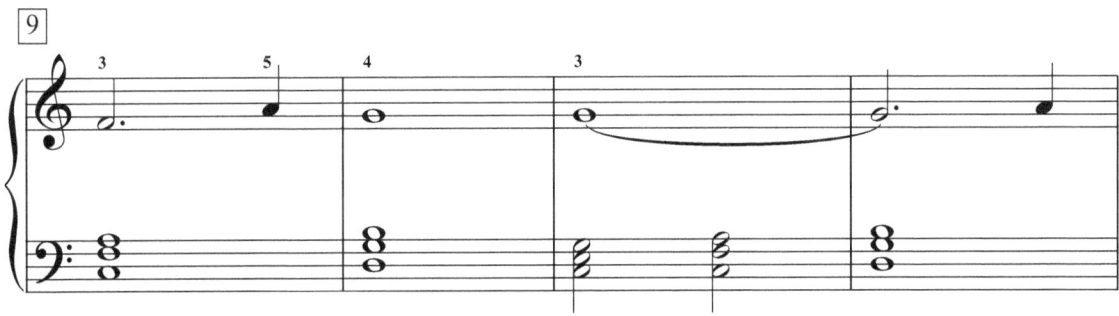
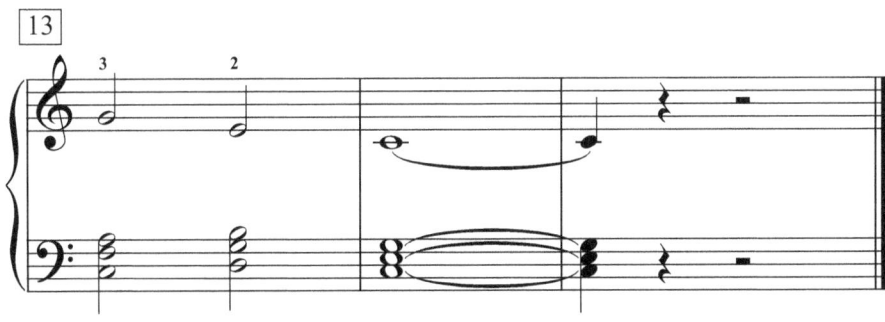

Primary Triads In F

*𝓟𝓮𝓭. means hold the damper pedal (one to the right) down. In the last bar, as you play just the low F, all the notes will sound together.

Primary Triads In G

When Harry Met Salary

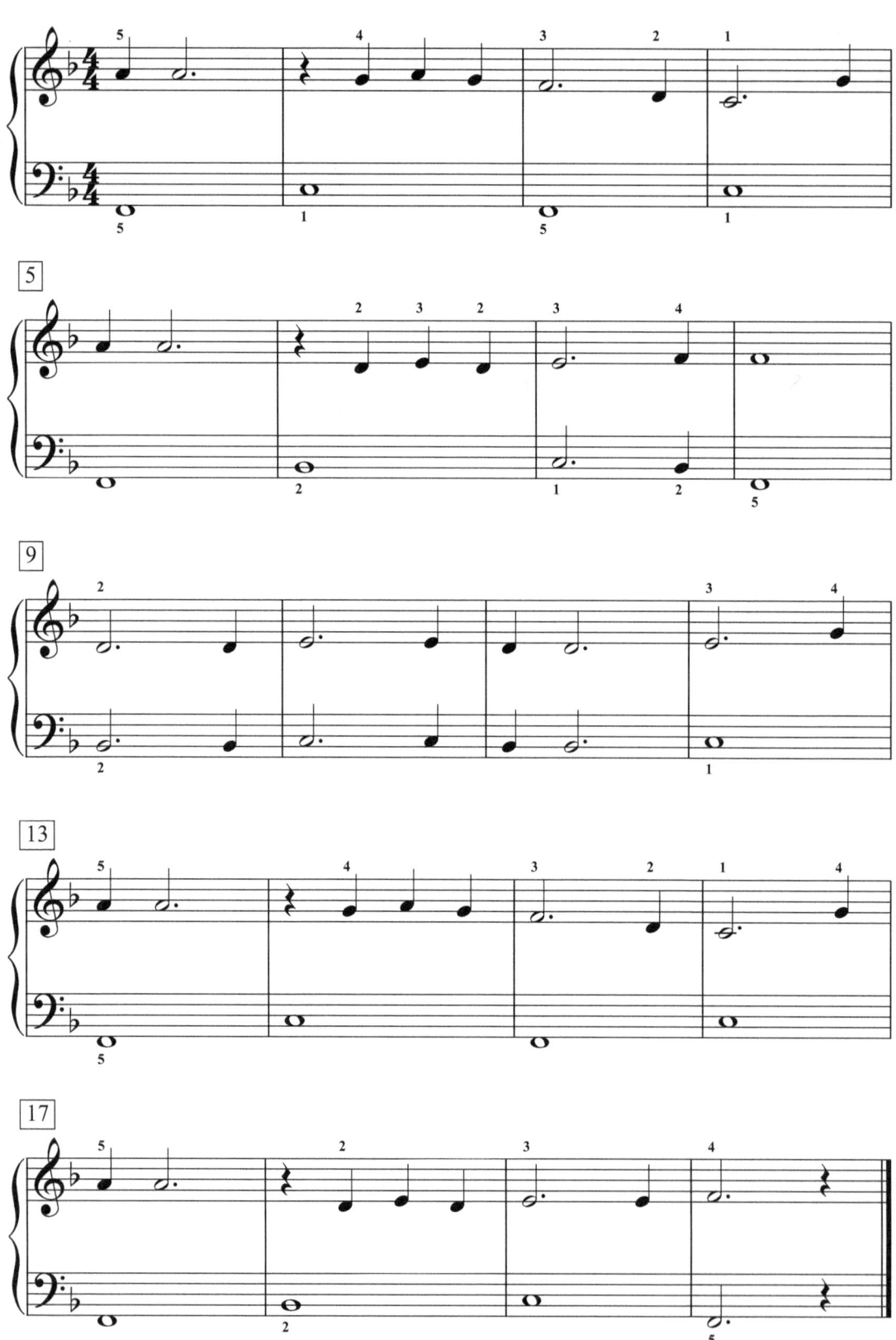

CHAPTER FOUR

Memory Check

Are you completely confident in being able to read the following notes?

If you are, great! You've almost reached your goal. If not, please go back and review before proceeding. Notes are your alphabetic key to a new language. Imagine trying to read words without knowing what a D or an N or an E is. That's when big time frustration enters the music-reading process, and is one of the reasons why people quit. So get over the hump. Learn the notes. Your rewards will be many.

New Notes: Treble Clef

B and C are the two highest notes you'll need to know for the purposes of this book. Here's how they look in context and by themselves:

B *sits on 1st ledger line* above staff

C is *2nd ledger line* above staff

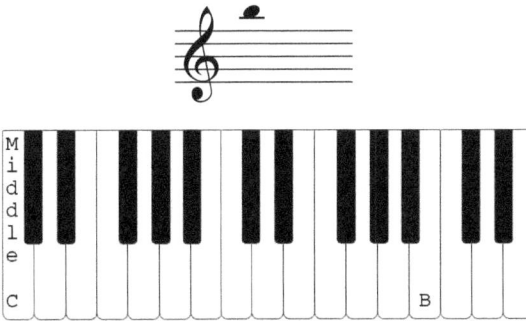

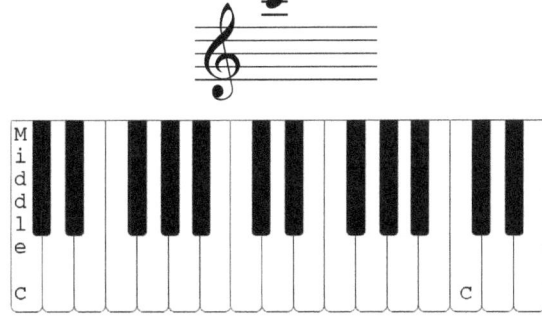

B is to the right of Black Group 3, to the left of C

C is to the right of B, to the left of D

Treble Clef - Two Octaves

New Notes: Bass Clef

D and C completes the lowest octave you'll need to know for this book. Here's how they look in context and by themselves.

D sits *below* 1st ledger line below the staff

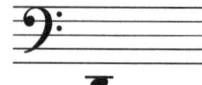

C is *on* the 2nd ledger line below the staff

Here are the notes at work together.

Bass Clef - Two Octaves

New Duration Symbols: Eighth Note and Rest, Dotted Quarter and Rest

You are going to be seeing the following new duration symbols for the rest of your musical life. The music you've read so far has necessarily been a little 'stiff.' With the introduction of these new symbols, much more varied music can be written. So let the party begin!

This is one eighth note

When you split a quarter note

into two equal parts,

you get two eighth notes.

In music terms

In math terms $\dfrac{1}{4} = \dfrac{1}{8} + \dfrac{1}{8}$

Symbolically

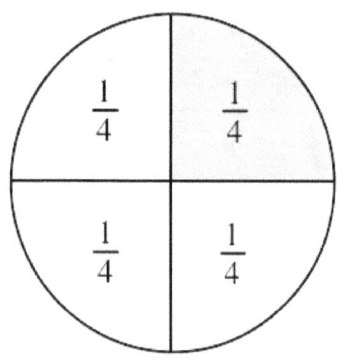 =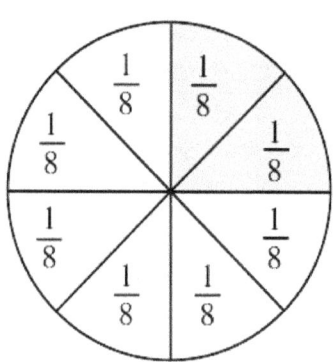

| $\dfrac{1}{4}$ | $\dfrac{1}{4}$ | $\dfrac{1}{4}$ | $\dfrac{1}{4}$ |

=

| $\dfrac{1}{8}$ | $\dfrac{1}{8}$ | $\dfrac{1}{8}$ | $\dfrac{1}{8}$ | $\dfrac{1}{8}$ | $\dfrac{1}{8}$ | $\dfrac{1}{8}$ | $\dfrac{1}{8}$ |

In terms of time passing by

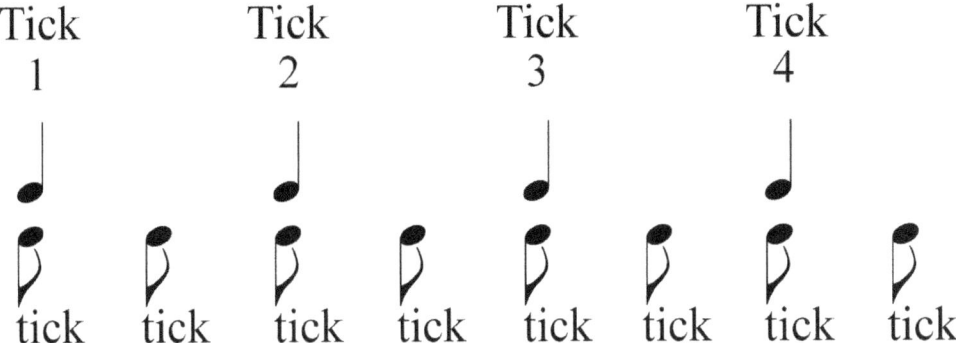

The traditional way to count music where eighth notes are the smallest values is to say

"one and two and three and four and"

It's represented on paper like this.

1 + 2 + 3 + 4 +

Here's how you'd superimpose this counting idea.

Another counting method would write numbers to the above example like this.

This is fine if you can remember and *feel* that '+' part of the pulse. For most beginners, the first example with all the 'ands' put in as place keepers is safer and keeps you from getting lost.

Beaming

When two or four eighth notes appear next to each other, rather than write

we write

in music for piano and most other instruments. The exception is traditional vocal music as in opera where they write out each note separately.

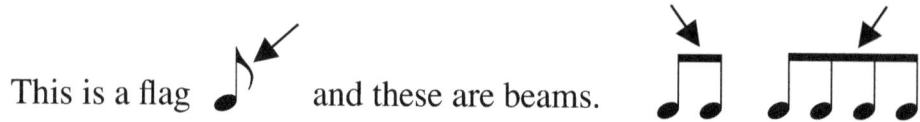

This is a flag and these are beams.

Beams make groups of notes easier to read. Flags are used when the eighth note has to stand alone rhythmically as in

Here's an example where eighth notes are beamed and not beamed.

Since we now have an eighth *note*, it follows that we'll need an eighth *rest*. Here it is ♪ and here's how it looks in context.

Stem direction for beamed eighth notes follows a 'majority rules' principle. Tie-breakers are decided by context.

Before more music with eighth notes and eighth rests appears, there is one more duration symbol to learn that very much goes with or complements the ♪ and 𝄾 . It's referred to as the DOTTED QUARTER and looks exactly as it sounds ♩. .

Remember the deal with the dot after a note? It adds half the value. So when you count the dotted quarter you say to yourself or out loud, "one and two." In context it looks like this.

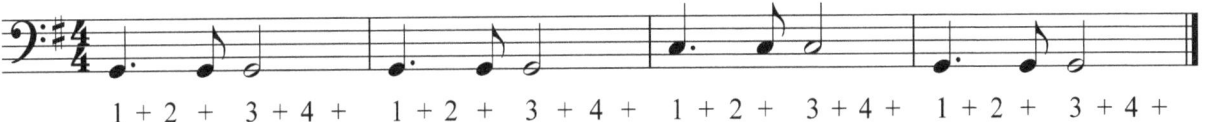

1 + 2 +   3 + 4 +   1 + 2 +   3 + 4 +   1 + 2 +   3 + 4 +   1 + 2 +   3 + 4 +

Put the eighth rest into the mix and this is what you get.

1 + 2 + 3 +   1 + 2 + 3   +   1 + 2 + 3 +

One more symbol and you're home free for the rest of this chapter.

Where there's smoke, there's fire. And where there's a dotted quarter note, there has to be a dotted quarter rest. This is it:

It's counted the same, of course, as a dotted quarter.

1 + 2

All these symbols take up the same amount of time.

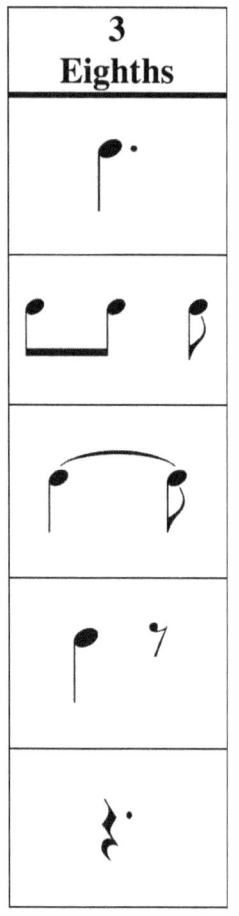

Bass and Melody Lines from Bach Chorales

The following six pages of music are extracted from four-part J. S. Bach Chorales. Now that you know eighth notes and dotted quarters, you can begin to play and enjoy some beautiful music such as this.

Bach's bass lines as well as his melodies - some of which are traditional - are a wonder to behold. By sight reading or practicing these lines, you'll be developing an understanding and appreciation of one of the reasons why baroque music sounds the way it does.

If you'd eventually like to see all four parts (soprano, alto, tenor, bass), refer to a book called 'Bach - Riemenschneider - 371 Harmonized Chorales and 69 Chorale Melodies with Figured Bass' published by G. Schirmer, Inc.

Chorale Bass Lines In F

Chorale Bass Lines In G

54

65

Chorale Melodies In F

224

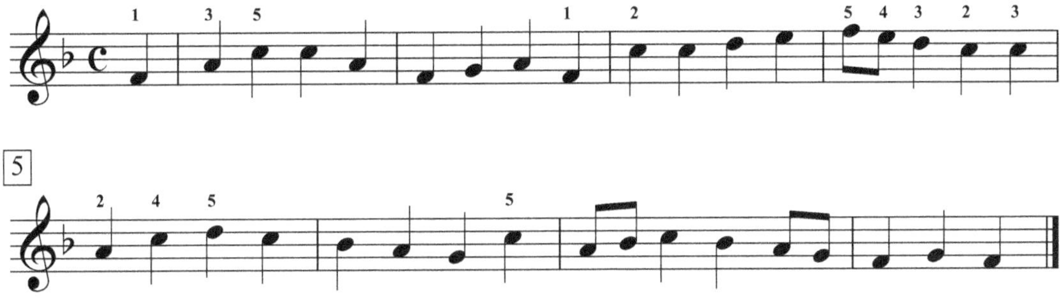

303

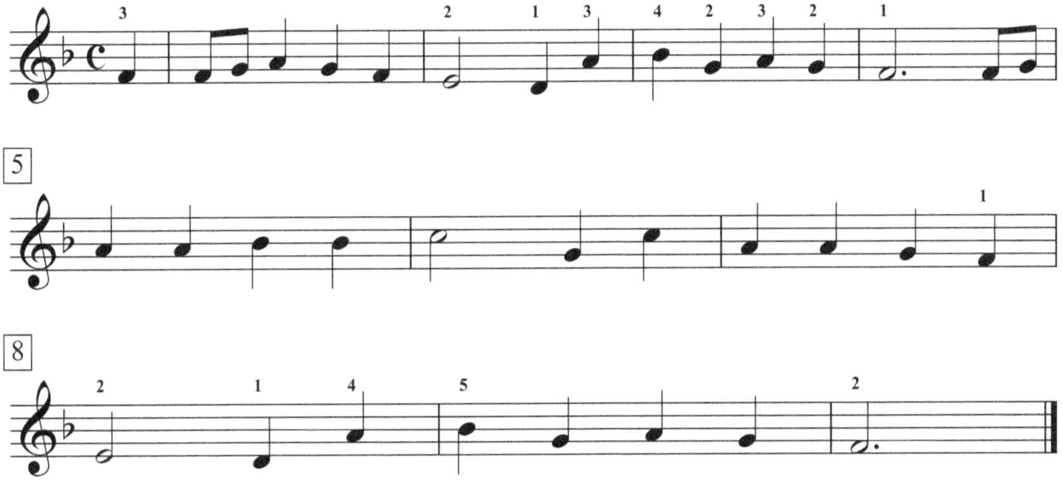

Chorale Melodies In G

9

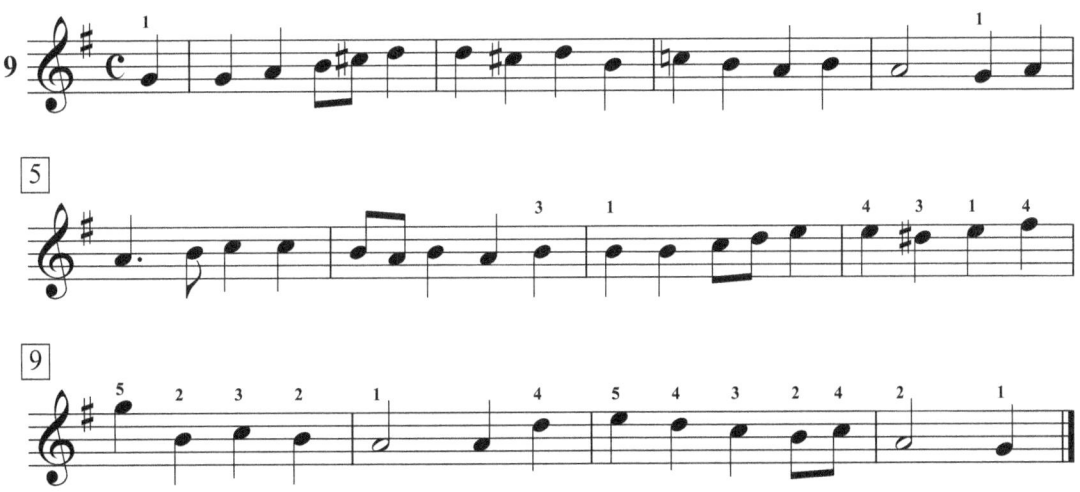

Interval Review

A quick review of intervals studied so far:

minor second = 1/2 step

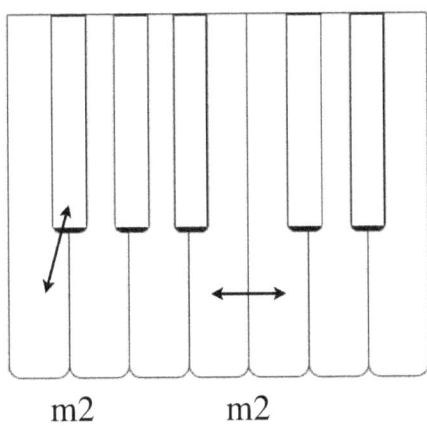

Major second = 1 step

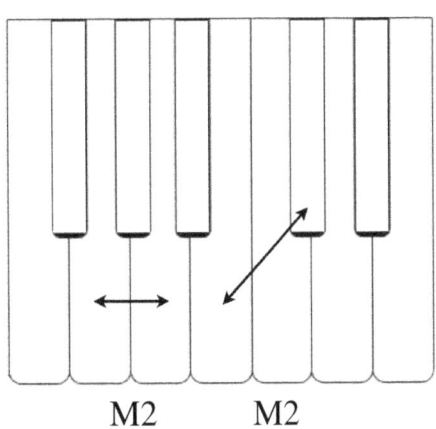

minor third = 1 1/2 steps

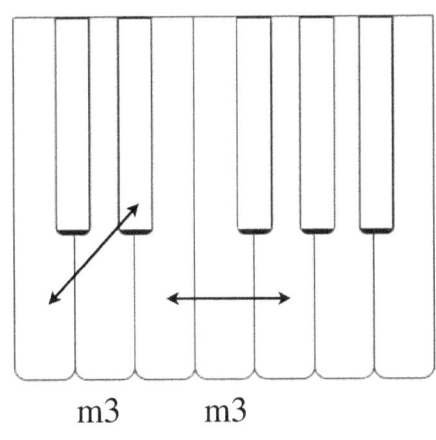

Major third = 2 steps

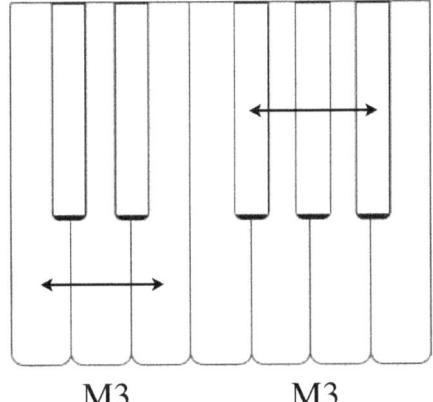

New Intervals: Perfect Fourth and Perfect Fifth, Augmented Fourth/Diminished Fifth

Perfect Fourth = 2 1/2 steps

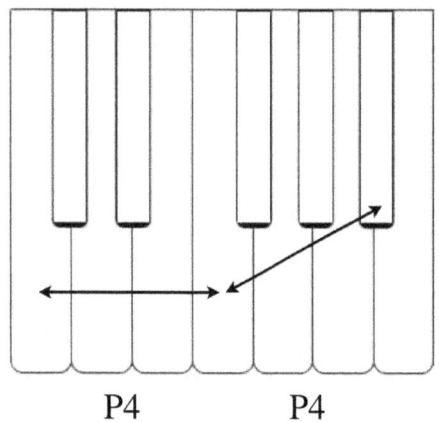

Augmented Fourth/Diminished Fifth = 3 steps

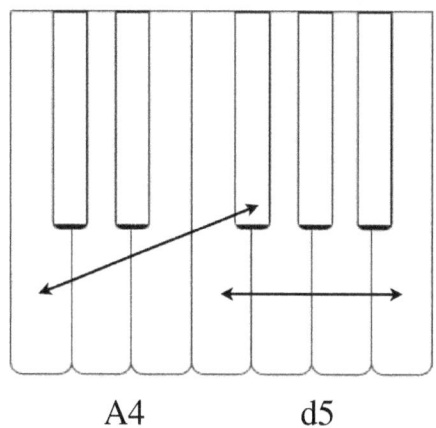

Perfect Fifth = 3 1/2 steps

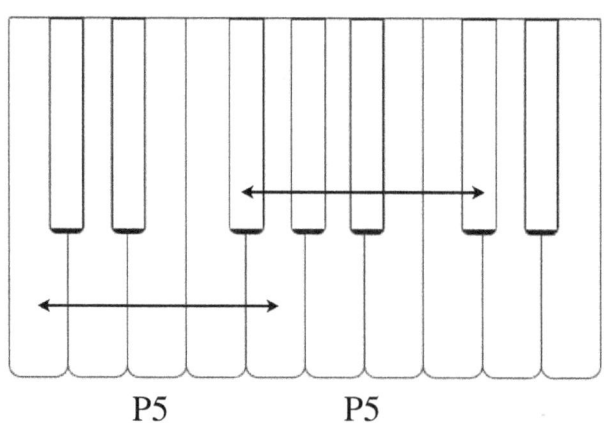

The applications of the perfect fourth, the augmented fourth and the diminished fifth will soon be seen. Suffice it to say that the P4 consists of two and a half steps, and the A4/d5/tritone of three whole steps.

The perfect fifth, which consists of three and a half steps, is useful to us because, by knowing 5^{ths}, we can logically figure out the sharps and flats that go with every major key through a system called the Circle of Fifths or the Cycle of Fifths.

The Circle of Fifths

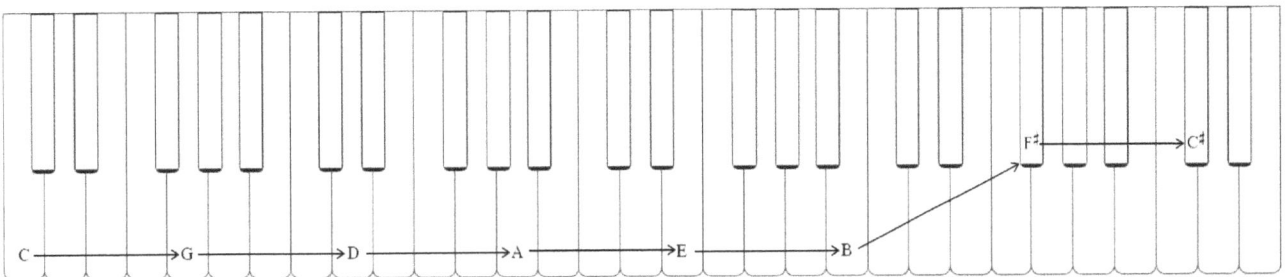

As it turns out, if you start on the C below middle C and go up a perfect 5th you come to G. If you construct a major scale starting on G (1 1 1/2 1 1 1 1/2), you end up with one sharp (F♯) in the scale. If you construct a major scale a perfect 5th above G on D, you end up with two sharps (F♯ and C♯). If you start a perfect 5th above D, which is A, and build a major scale, you get three sharps (F♯, C♯ and G♯). Guess what? This system continues in the same way up to C♯ which has seven sharps.

Key	#	Sharps	Signature
C	0	0	
G	1	F♯	
D	2	F♯, C♯	
A	3	F♯, C♯, G♯	
E	4	F♯, C♯, G♯, D♯	
B	5	F♯, C♯, G♯, D♯, A♯	
F♯	6	F♯, C♯, G♯, D♯, A♯, E♯	
C♯	7	F♯, C♯, G♯, D♯, A♯, E♯, B♯	

The same principle, going *down* by fifths, reveals the flat keys.

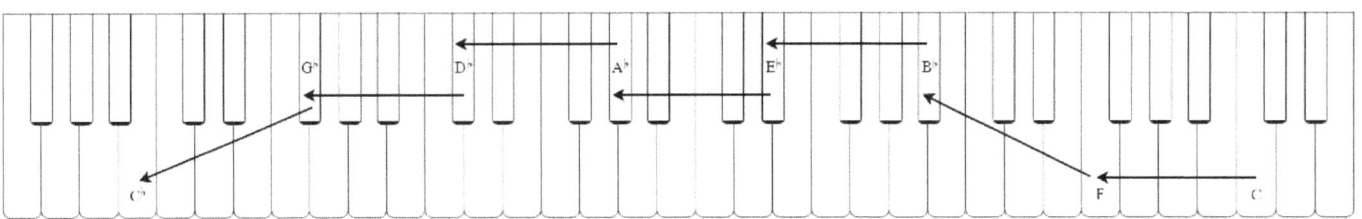

C	0	0	
F	1	B♭	
B♭	2	B♭, E♭	
E♭	3	B♭, E♭, A♭	
A♭	4	B♭, E♭, A♭, D♭	
D♭	5	B♭, E♭, A♭, D♭, G♭	
G♭	6	B♭, E♭, A♭, D♭, G♭, C♭	
C♭	7	B♭, E♭, A♭, D♭, G♭, C♭, F♭	

A convenient way to place all this information in a small amount of space is the following diagram; hence the name, THE CIRCLE OF FIFTHS.

Diagram of the Circle of Fifths

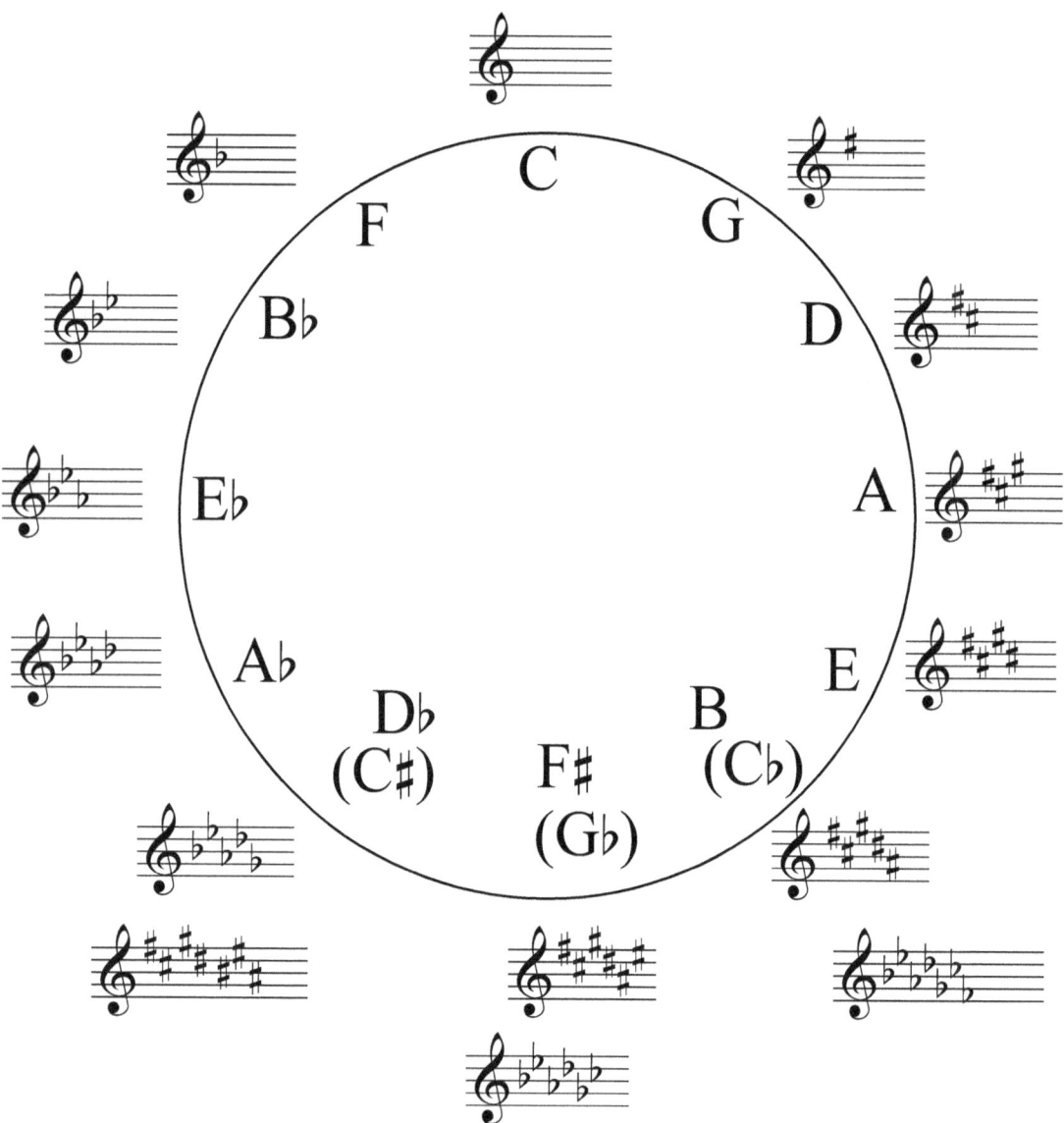

Enharmonics, Part I

When we talked about naming the black keys, we were already talking about enharmonics. G♭ and F♯ - the same note – are enharmonics. D♭ and C♯, B and C♭ – all are examples of ENHARMONICS: different spellings of the same note.

Why be in the key of G♭ instead of F♯? The answer for now is 'What is easier for the player to read?' The key of B has 5 sharps. The key of C♭ has 7 flats. B is easier to read than C♭. There are other considerations we'll get into in the future.

Sachiyo's Tunes

One summer day I was teaching this information to a class by going up or down the piano by perfect fifths as I have just done for you. As I asked everyone to try this out on their own pianos, from the back of the room, I heard these little tunes:

and

They came from one of my students, Sachiyo. She had figured out a way to remember the order of keys from the circle of fifths in a way I had never heard or read about before. With her method you don't have to go up or down over four octaves. Her idea is very compact so I pass these clever little tunes on to you - courtesy of Sachiyo.

New Scales: D & B♭

Now that you've just seen the big picture - all the major keys displayed on the circle of fifths - here is your goal. For the purposes of this text, you are asked to learn C, G, D, A, E and B for the sharp keys, and F, B♭, E♭, A♭, and D♭ for the flat keys. If you'd like to learn F♯ and C♯, G♭ and C♭ they are written out in the appendix.

So far, you know three scales C, F and G. Today we move into D and B♭.

To find out what notes are in the D major scale, start on the note D and apply the formula:

You should end up with these notes:

Since the key signature consists of two sharps, F♯ and C♯, it's written like this:

Once again there is good news. The fingering for D is *exactly* like C. You just have to get used to playing F♯s and C♯s.

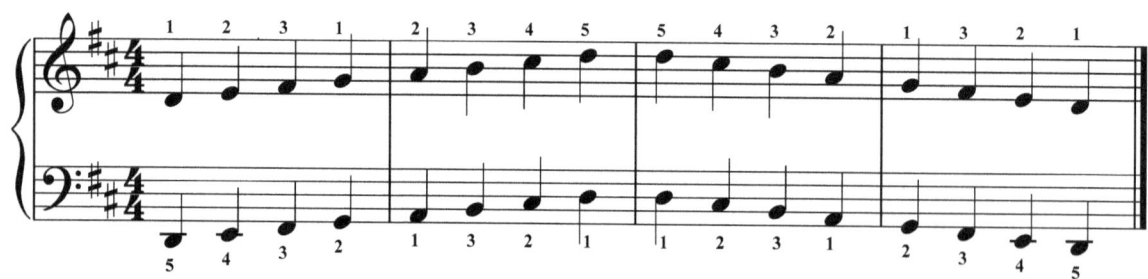

Here are the primary chords that go with the D major scale followed by some pieces in the new key.

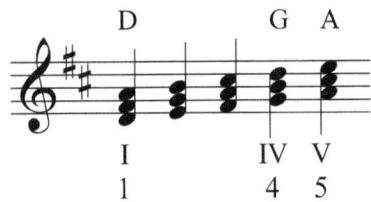

Tortoise Wins

Sunlight on Water

Wild Party

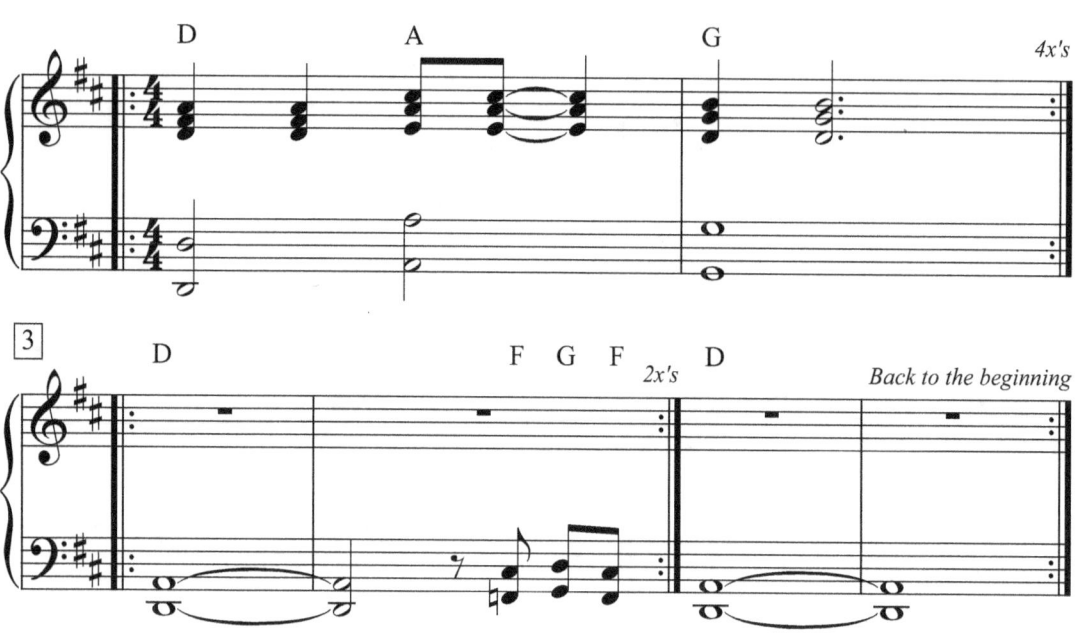

Bashful Ballerina

* Since most hands can't stretch an octave using 2 to 5 as a fingering, a technique called 'Finger Substitution' exists for situations like this. Play the lower E with 2, then put your thumb on that E. You're now fine to reach for 5.

Waltz of the Weird

Hollywood Rain

The other new scale in this chapter is B♭. Once again we'll superimpose the formula for a major scale starting on B♭. This is what we get:

Here's how the key signature looks:

Because this scale starts on a black key, the *fingering* for the right hand is *very different* from what you've experienced so far.

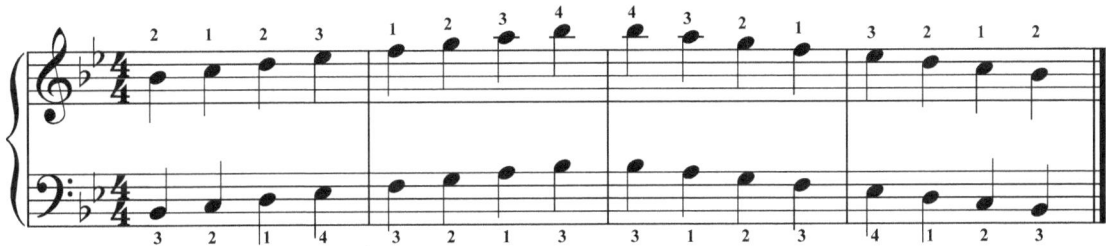

These are the primary triads that go with B♭ major.

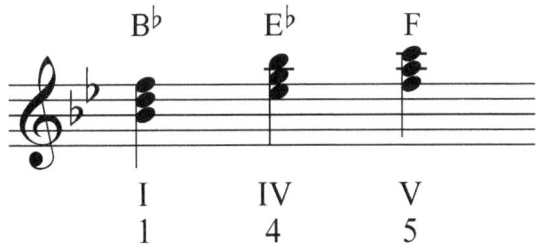

Bonus Notes

I said right from the start that the goal was 30 notes. There are, however, 4 bonus notes that give the pianist a lot of 'extra mileage' compared to the effort required to learn them. For instance, to write the B♭ scale an octave lower than just written, you need the B (in this case, with a flat sign) below middle C. No big deal - it looks like this:

The other 3 notes to know are A, G, and F.

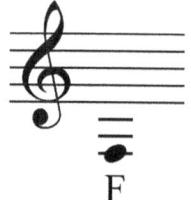

I give these to you because, when it comes to voicing chords for the right hand, these notes add richness to the sound. For instance, this F chord

 or this one

sounds much fuller than this one.

She, Who Can Do No Wrong

Holiday Bells

Hearty Sailors

Gigi and Sadie

Techno Prisoners

Simple and Compound Meter

Now that we have an understanding of eighth notes, we can demonstrate and analyze various meters. Meter, as a reminder, is how the beats or pulses are grouped into (usually equal) measures. The time signature reveals the meter, and when any group of musicians get together to play some music for the first time, the first question is often, "What's the feel?" which is today's way of asking, "What's the meter?"

The most commonly used meter is 4/4 and a shortcut symbol has evolved over the centuries that looks like this: **C** . We call this "common time" but **C** *does not* stand for the word 'common.' Briefly, six hundred years ago, circles and half circles symbolized time signatures.

SIMPLE METER means that *the basic pulse* – in this case, the quarter note, *can be divided in two*. Remember how we counted this figure?

1 + 2 + 3 + 4 +

"One and" (1 +) is this subdivision into the 2 units of time we're talking about.

We talk about simple meter in terms of simple duple, simple triple, and simple quadruple. Here are the simplest, most commonly used examples of each. For examples of other less common meters, see appendix.

Simple duple

1 + 2 +   1 + 2 +   1 + 2 +   1 + 2 +

Simple triple

Simple quadruple

COMPOUND METER means *each main pulse will be subdivided into 3*. Let's let a famous cartoon theme demonstrate.

If you've ever watched American TV, you may have heard the theme to 'I'm Popeye the Sailor Man.'

> I'm Popeye the Sailor Man
> I'm Popeye the Sailor Man
> I'm strong to the finich 'cause
> I eats me spinach
> I'm Popeye the Sailor Man.

Bad grammar and invented rhymes aside, the underlying pulses of this memorable little tune are felt in *groups of three* – the essence of compound time. Other ways to think of it are

- the beat unit is always a dotted note
- you can always divide the top number of the time signature by 3
- the top number will either be a 6, 9 or 12.

Here's how 'Popeye' looks written out.

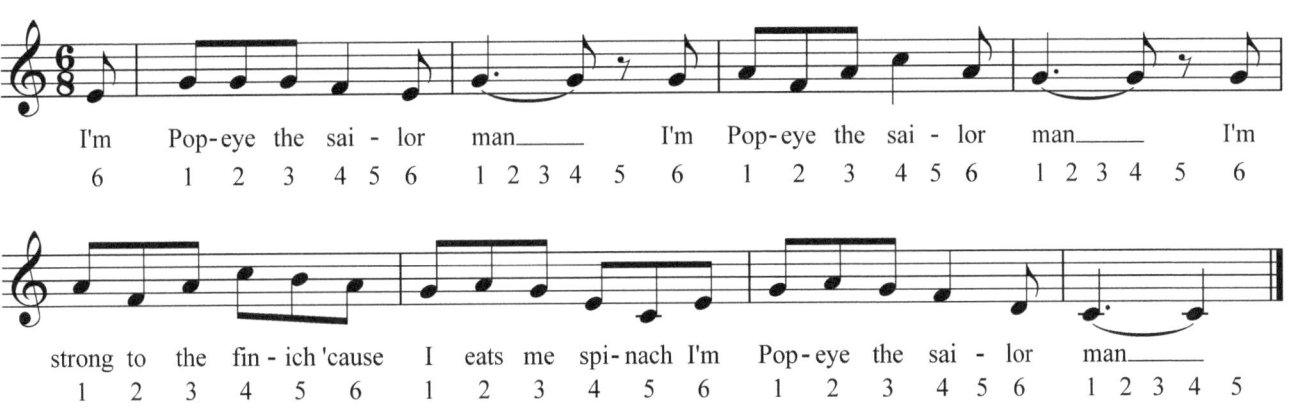

Do you feel how the repeating cycles of 1-2-3 1-2-3, 1-2-3 1-2-3 give this $\frac{6}{8}$ piece the feeling of compound time? That 1-2-3 is the basic pulse and there are two of them per measure.

The more commonly used compound time signatures are $\frac{6}{8}$, $\frac{12}{8}$, and some $\frac{9}{8}$. If you've ever listened to Blues or 50's Rock & Roll you've heard $\frac{12}{8}$.

Baby, I Love You

9/8 has a few examples.

Beautiful Dreamer

Obtainable Goal

Jesu, Joy of Man's Desiring

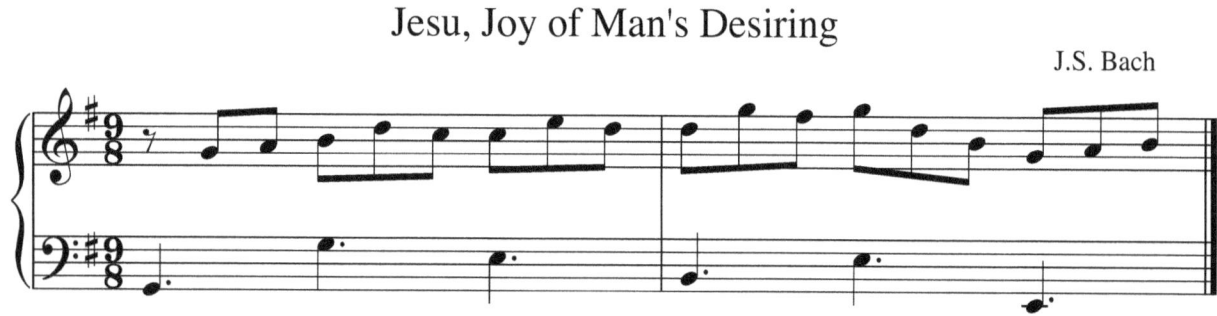

Ralph In The Clouds

Love In The 50's

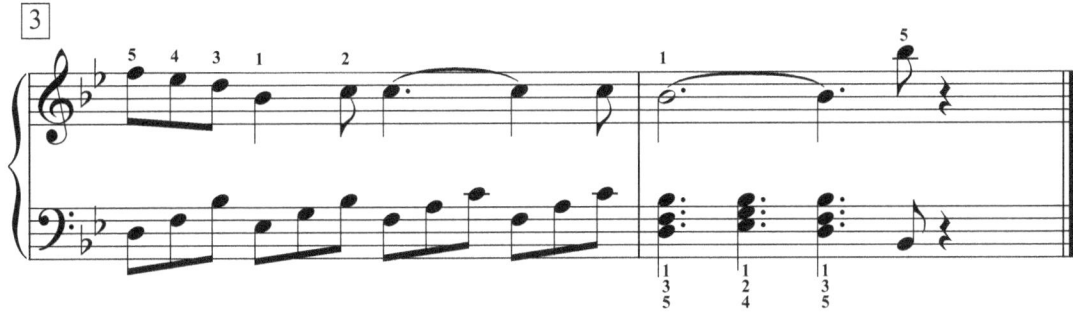

Where And Why

Chord Meditation

The Diaper Changing Blues

Chords So Far

Let's take an inventory of the chords you know.

C F G B♭ D A E♭

Seven major chords give you the ability to play I-IV-V progressions in five keys.

C	F	G
F	B♭	C
G	C	D
D	G	A
B♭	E♭	F

Make sure you know the notes in these chords thoroughly.

Primary Triads In Five Keys

Chord In Right Hand, Single Note In Bass

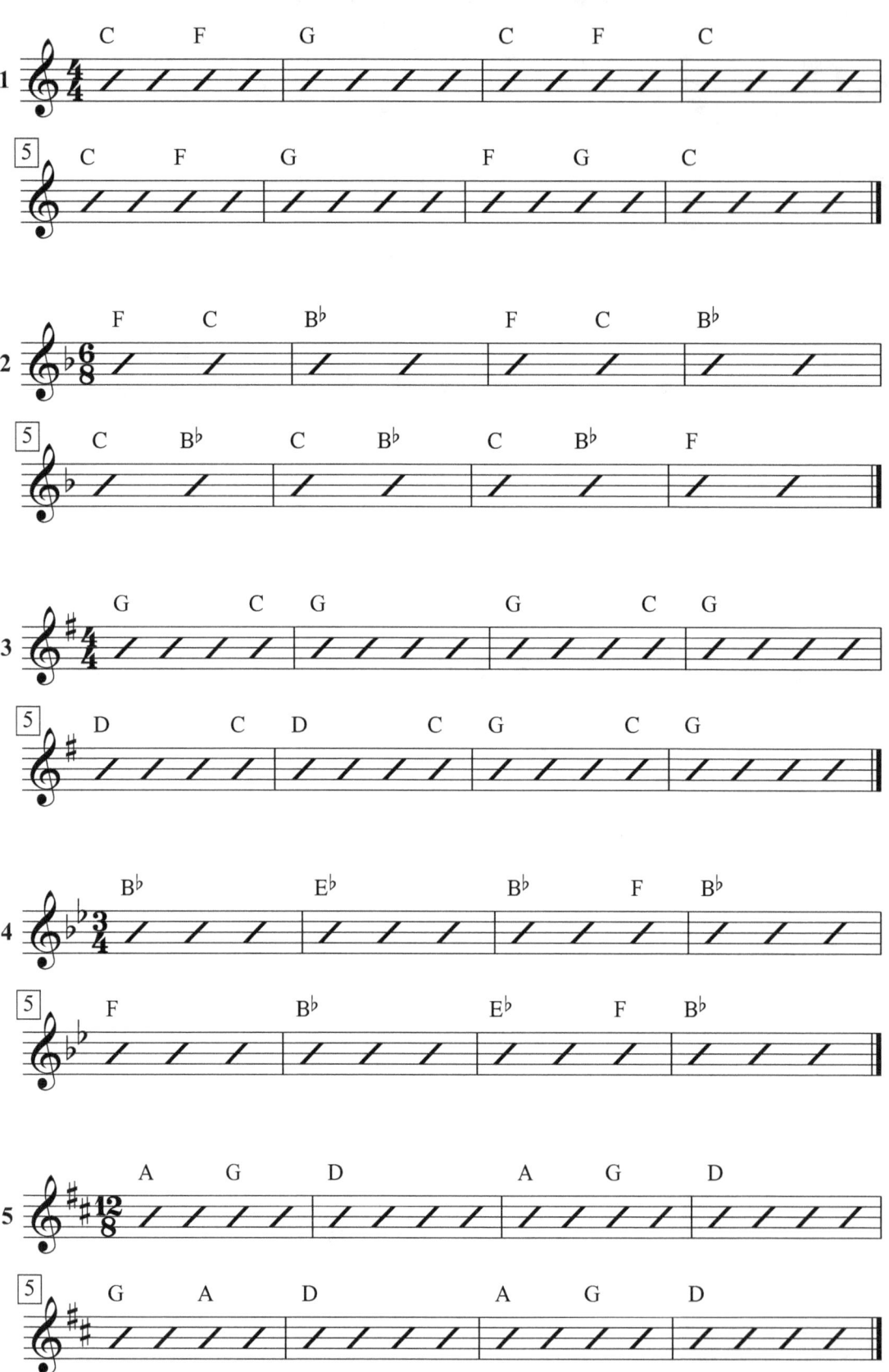

Nashville Number Charts Using Primary Triads

C: 1   4   1   5
    1   4   1/4   1
    5   1   5   1
    1   4   1/5   1

D: 4   5   1   1
    1   4   5   5
    4   5   1   1
    1   4   5   5
    4   5   1   1
    4   5   1   1
    4   5   1   1

F: 1   1   5   1
    1   1   4   5
    1   1   4   4
    1   1   5   1

B♭: 5   1   5   1
    4   4   5   5
    1   5/4 1   1
    4   4   5   5
    1   5/4 1   1
    4   4   1   1
    5   1   5   1
    4   4   5/4 1
    5/4 1   5/4 1

G: 1   5   1   5
    4   5   1   1
    1   5   1   5
    4   5   1   1
    4   5   4   5
    4   4   5   5
    1   5   1   5
    4   5   1   1

One Way To Interpret A Chord Chart

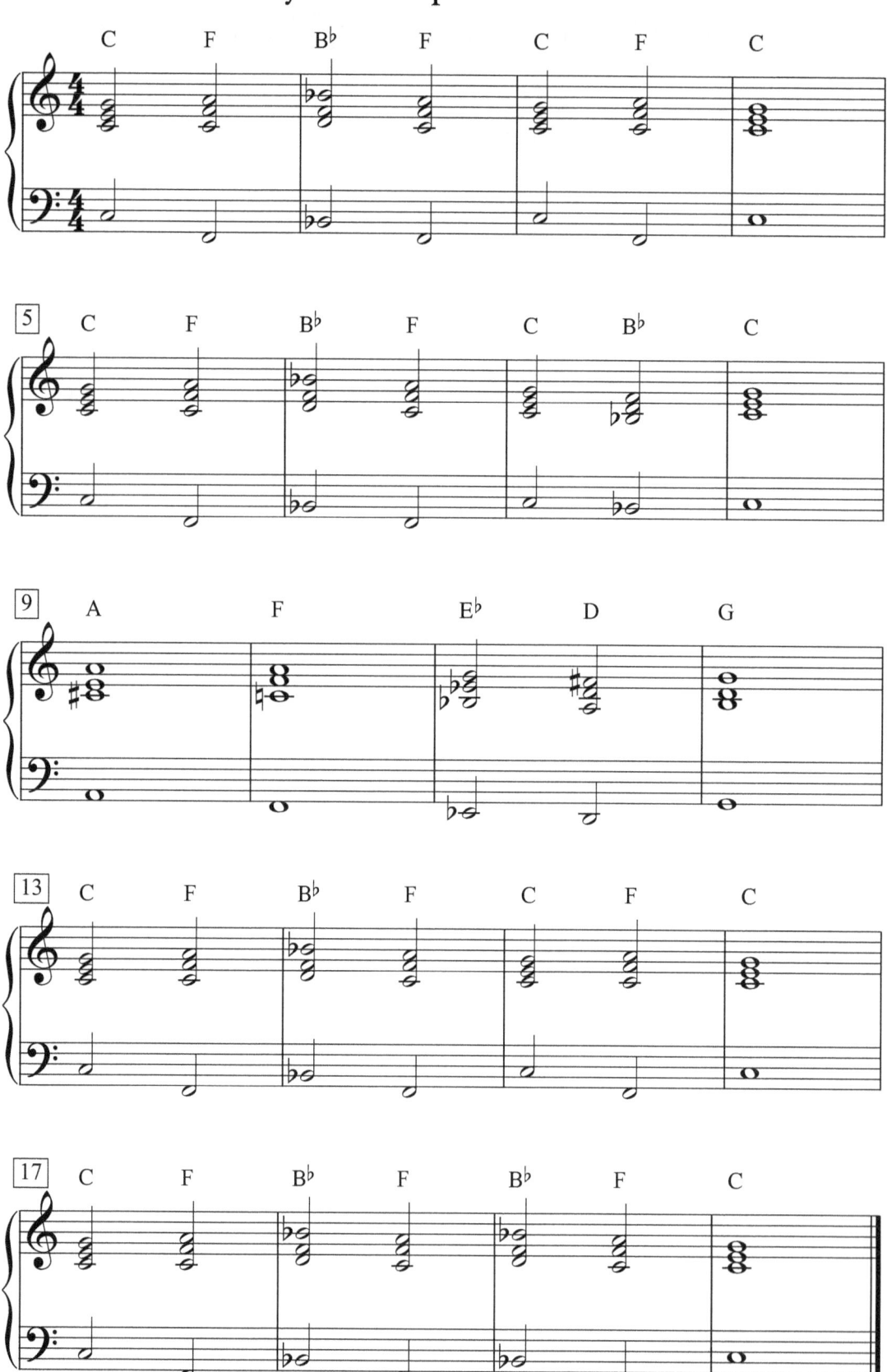

Rhythm Gym

Questions

Q: Why would anybody in their right mind, write music in the key of C♭ instead of B, or in C♯ instead of D♭?

A: Good question. The easy answer is that, in general, you are right. Why have to read 7 flats when you can read 5 sharps, or why read 7 sharps when you can read 5 flats? This generality will almost always apply to piano music because the piano is a fixed pitch instrument.

In the case of stringed instruments, when the player places their finger on a string to create a pitch, there is a tiny bit of difference between a C flat and a B natural. Some composers who wish to exploit that difference would then write in the more difficult to read key.

Q: Why do we have chord voicings? Can't we just play the primary triads in root position like D-F♯-A, G-B-D, A-C♯-E?

A: That's like asking, "Why do we mix peanuts or raisins with chocolate?" For variety, that's why! The basic triad C-E-G takes on a variety of tonal shadings when the order of the notes is mixed up. Try it. C-E-G to E-G-C to G-C-E, or how about C-G-E?

Q: I'm a little confused about the time signature's meaning in simple and compound time. In simple time the top number of the time signature means – let's use 4/4 for an example – there are 4 beats in a measure. But in something like 6/8 time, the 6 doesn't really mean that there are 6 beats in every measure. What gives?

A: Very good question. When you have compound time, the top number of the time signature has to be divided by 3 to tell you how many main pulses there are per bar. That means that 6/8 time actually has 2 main pulses per bar, not 6. 12/8 would have 4 strong pulses and 9/8 would have 3.

There are certain principles in music that *you just have to know*. For instance, the whole rest in 4/4 time equals 4 beats. The whole rest in 3/4 time that looks exactly the same equals 3 beats.

Guided Practice

When the notes of a chord are repeated - either at a higher octave or as in this case, up and down, you have what are called *arpeggios*.

For the 'Unchained Melody' excerpt start by getting used to the rolling effect that the left hand gives with the 1-2-3, 1-2-3 rhythm of compound time. With your left hand 5th finger on D, you'll find the natural place for your thumb will actually be in the air, away from the wooden lip of the piano. That's o.k. That's where it wants to be for a moment.

As your 3rd finger plays F♯ and your 2nd finger plays A, there should be a natural *pivoting to the right* as your thumb seeks out D. Same thing on the way down the arpeggio; your hand should pull to the left.

Practice the six note pattern of bar 1 by itself until you almost don't have to think about it anymore and your hand feels like it's on 'automatic pilot.'

To make a smooth transition to the B of bar two requires you to keep your 3rd finger on the last F♯ of bar one until your hand swivels down to play that B. This is a principle called LEGATO, meaning 'connected.' If you didn't play with this legato technique, your playing would sound 'choppy.'

The transition to bar 4 is a little harder because you have to remember to substitute 3 for the more natural 4 on D. You have to do this because 4 on D to 5 on G of the next bar is awkward, and it would be difficult to achieve legato with that fingering.

To get to the A at the beginning of bar five, the 4th and 5th fingers almost squeeze together (you may feel them brush each other) as the 3rd finger plays C♯ and then is the pivot point of the hand as 2 and thumb swivel into place to play E and A.

To make the transition from the last C♯ of bar five to the 1st D of bar six requires that you simply lift up your hand and put it back down. For a beginner, trying to make those notes sound legato is too painful and awkward for your hand. So for now, just pick up your hand less than an inch and put it back down. The rest of this excerpt for the left hand has already been explained.

The right hand is the easy part. If you put your 3rd finger on the starting note D, as the music indicates, you'll be fine.

Watch out at bar five for the tendency to want to play the C♯ with your 3rd finger. That would back you into a corner so remember to use 2 on C♯.

The only other thing to remember is that at bar seven you're going to, once again, pick up your hand after you play D to then play the F♯ below. This is O.K. for a beginner. Eventually you'll learn a fingering technique called 'substitution.' For now, what you're doing is fine.

Unchained Melody
from the Motion Picture UNCHAINED

Lyric by Hy Zaret
Music by Alex North
Arranged by Jay Snyder

*New note = D above middle C

© 1955 (Renewed) FRANK MUSIC CORP.
This arrangement © 2009 FRANK MUSIC CORP
All Rights Reserved
Reprinted by permission of Hal Leonard Corporation

Music for Sight Reading and Practice

Simple Gifts

A Lover's Concerto

Words and Music by
Sandy Linzer and Denny Randell
Arranged by Jay Snyder

© 1965 (Renewed 1993) SCREEN GEMS-EMI MUSIC INC.
This arrangement © 2009 SCREEN GEMS-EMI MUSIC INC.
All Rights Reserved   International Copyright Secured   Used by Permission
Reprinted by permission of Hal Leonard Corporation

Lovers Of Simplicity

Mexican Folk Dance

Appendix 1

Scales
&
Primary Triads

C major
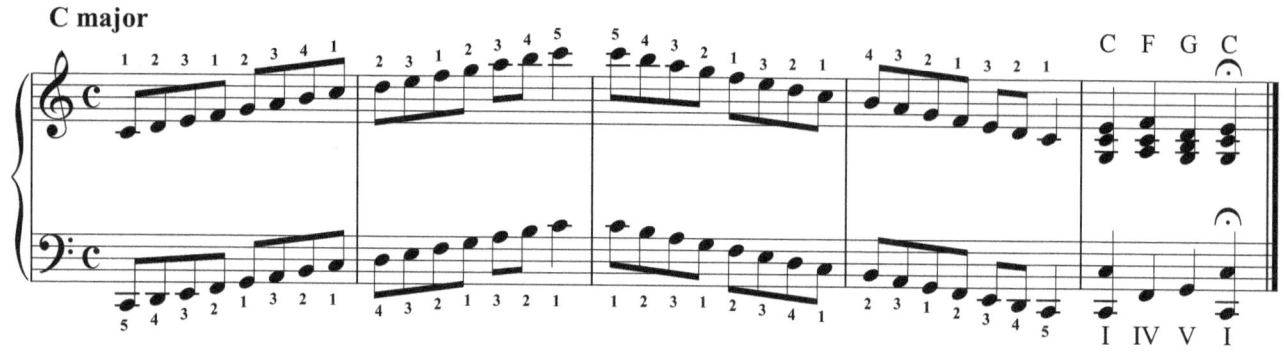

A natural minor

A harmonic minor

A melodic minor

G major
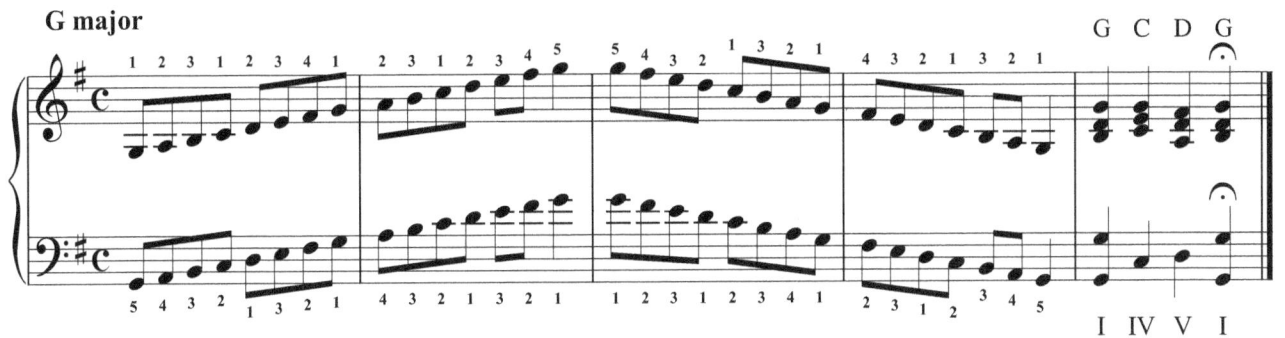

E natural minor
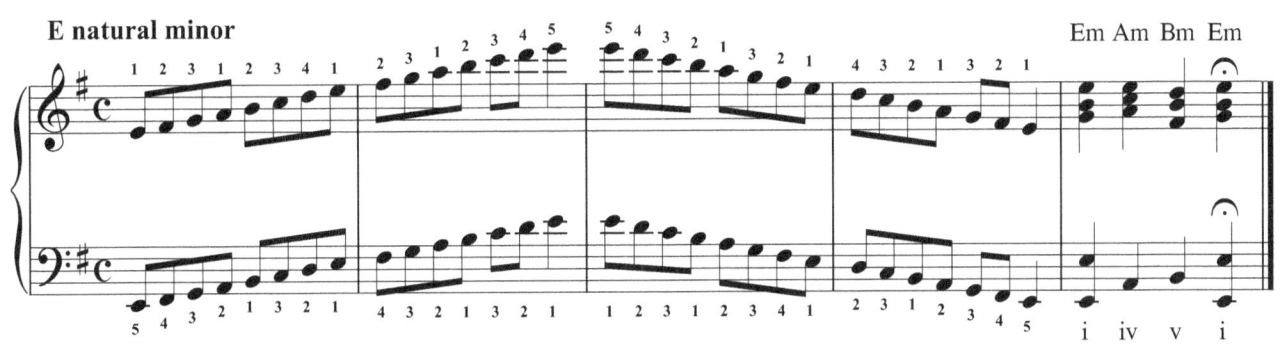

E harmonic minor
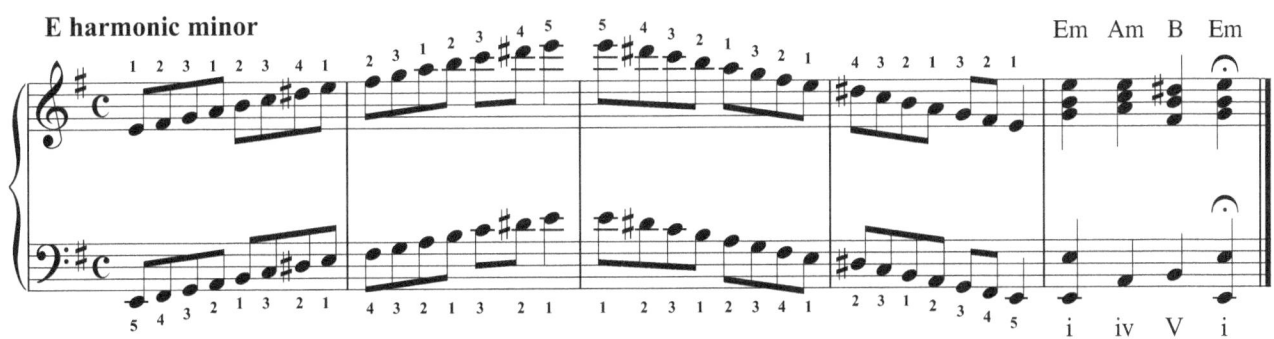

E melodic minor
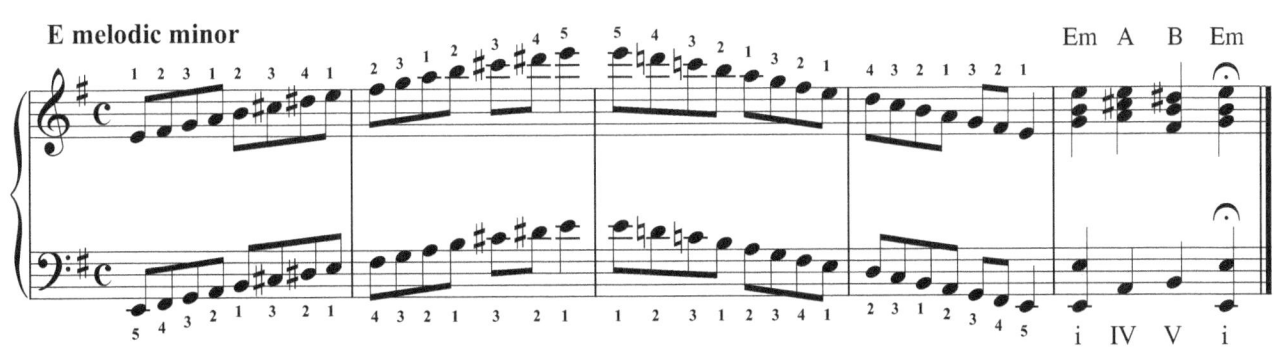

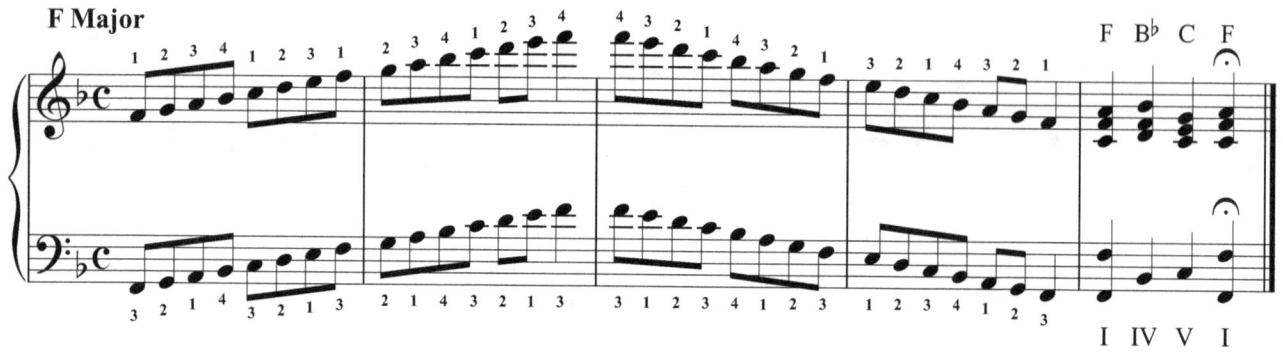

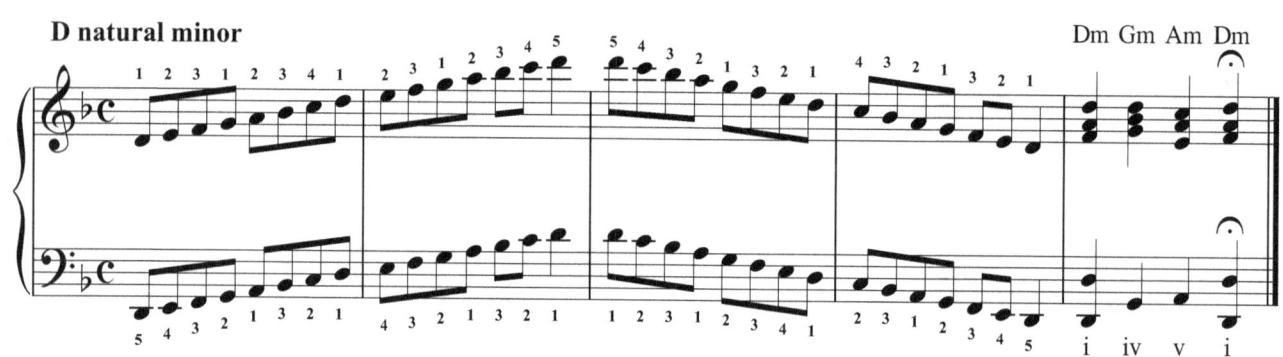

B♭ major

G natural minor

G harmonic minor

G melodic minor

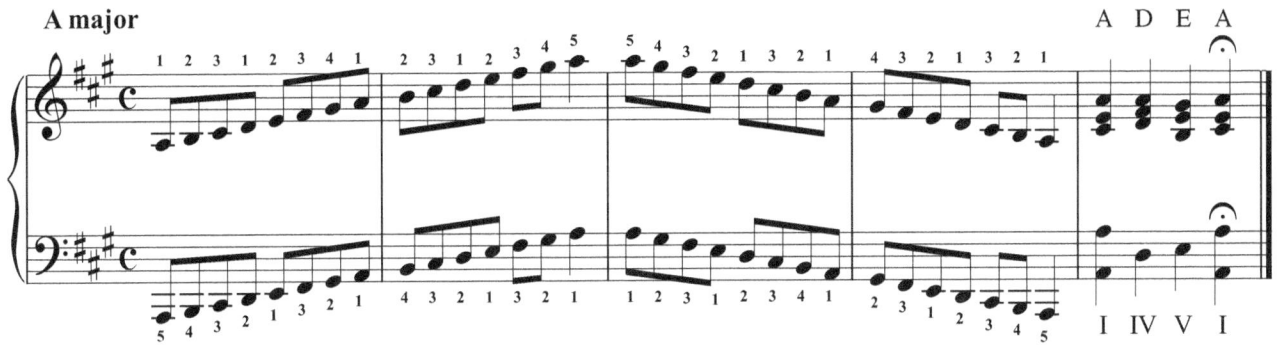
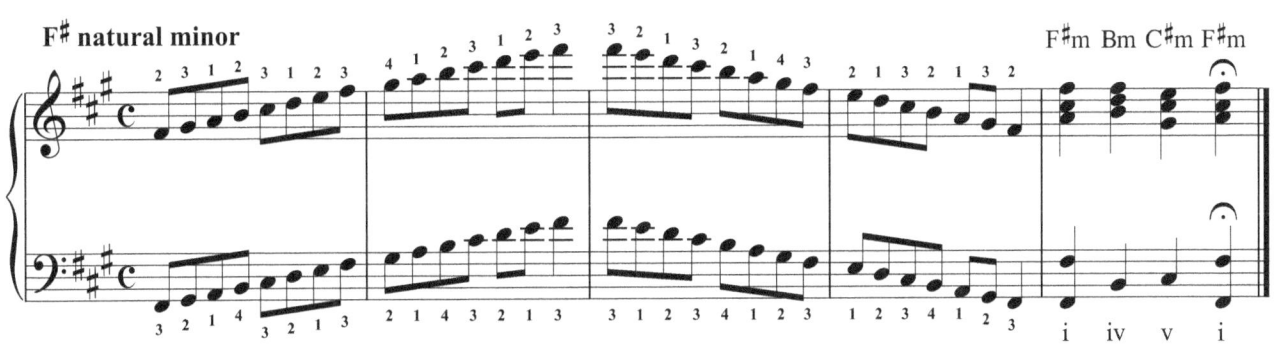

E♭ major

C natural minor

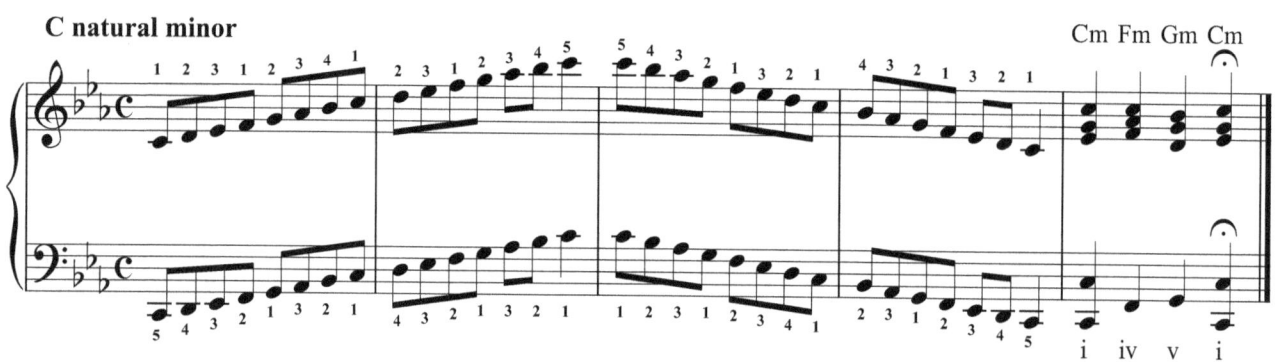

C harmonic minor

C melodic minor

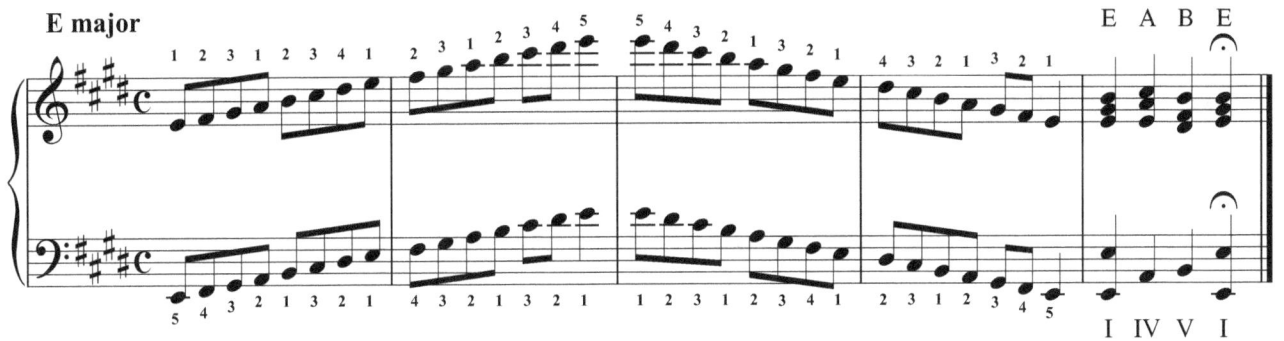

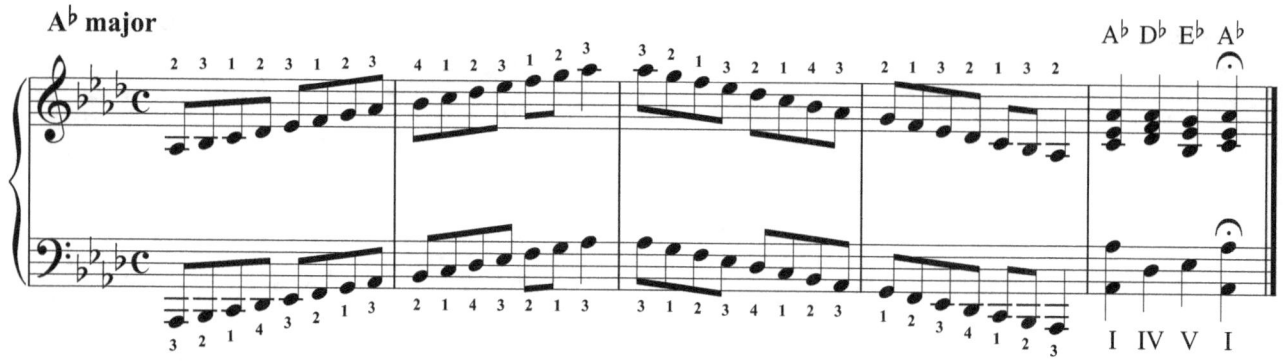
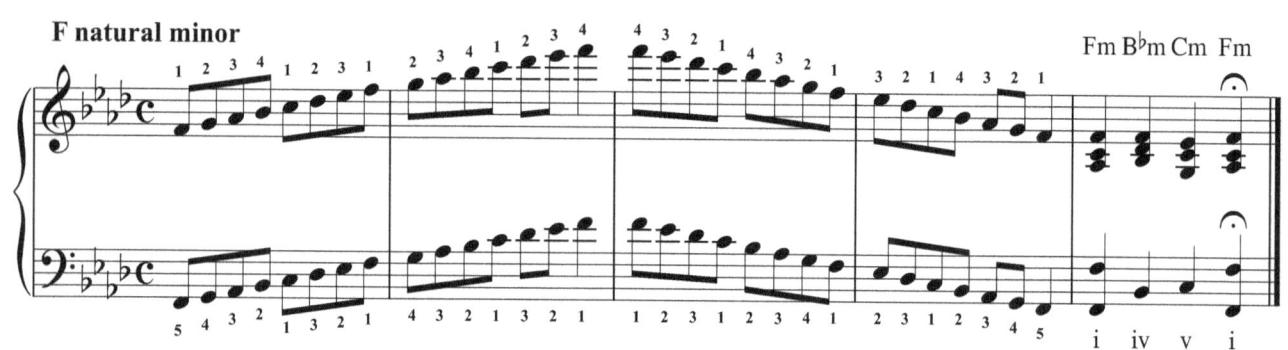
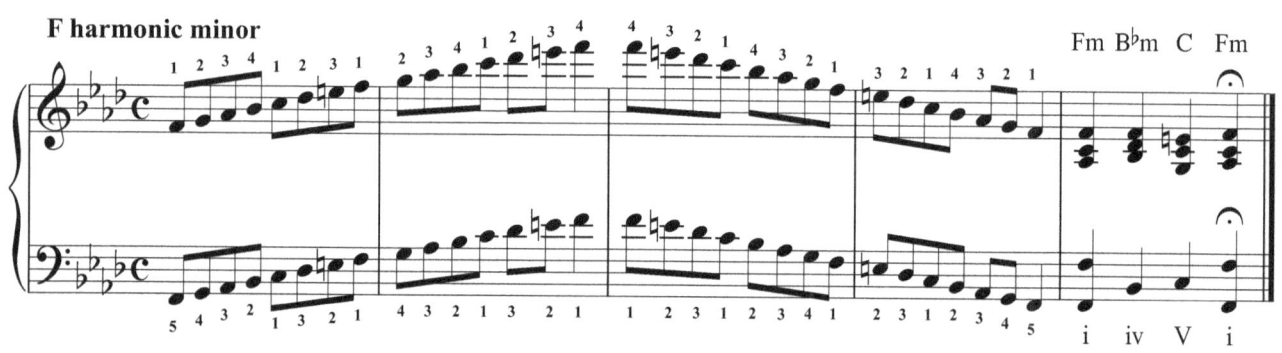

170

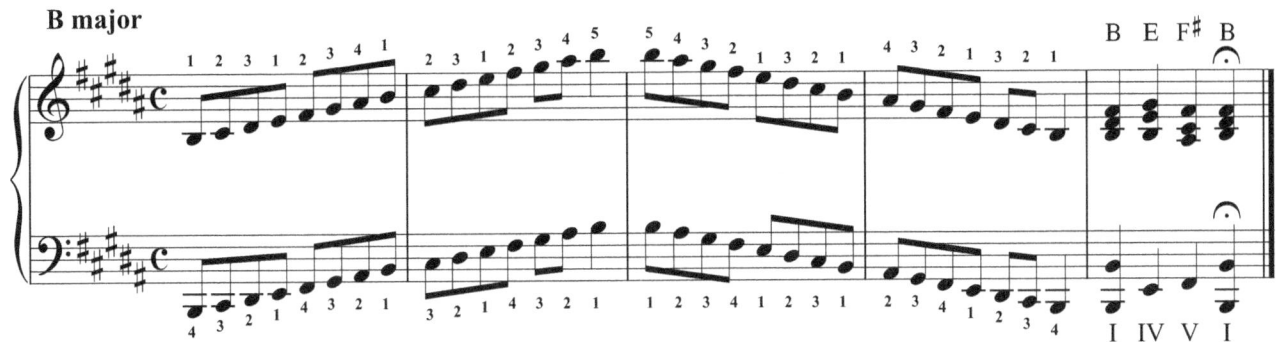
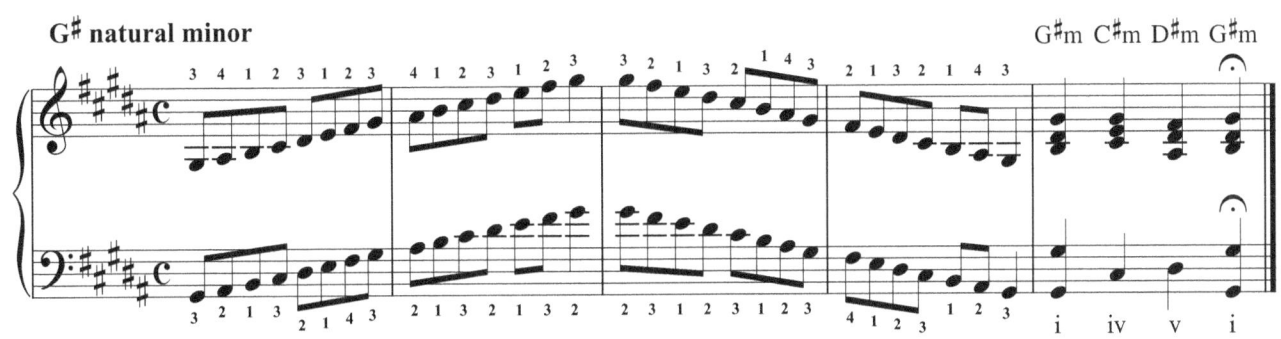

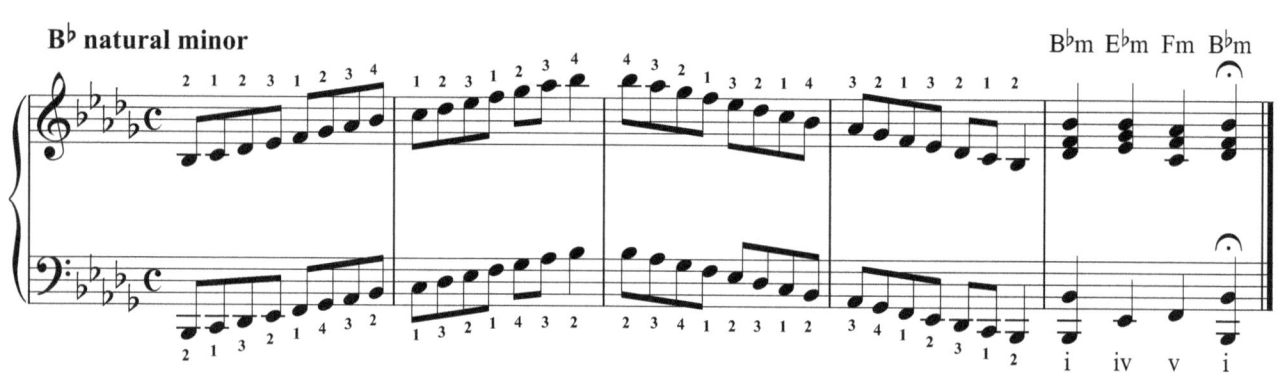

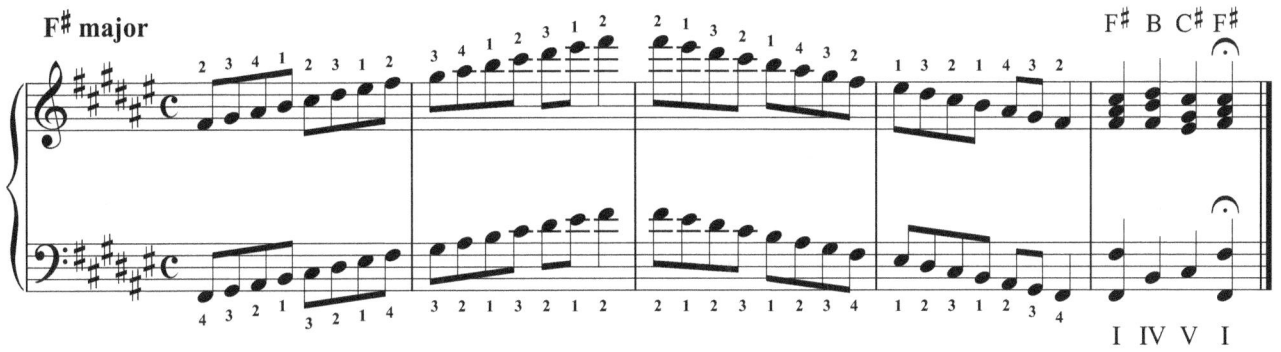

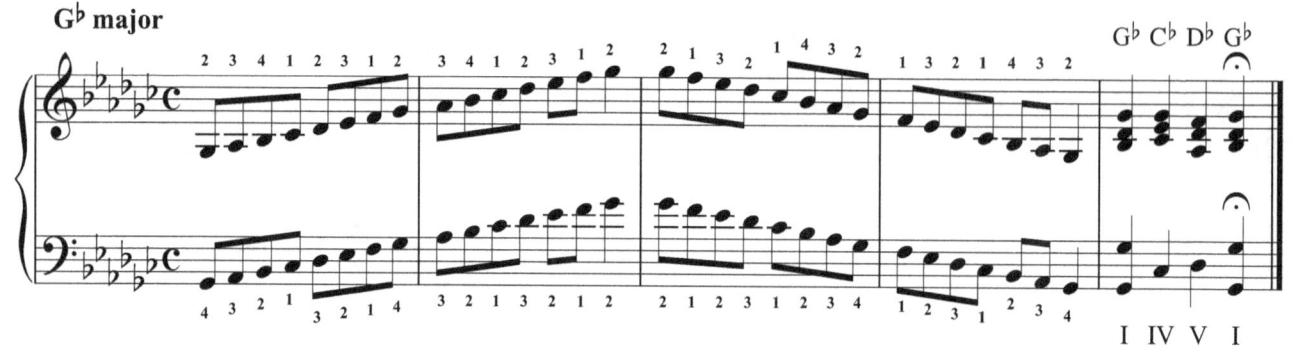

C# major

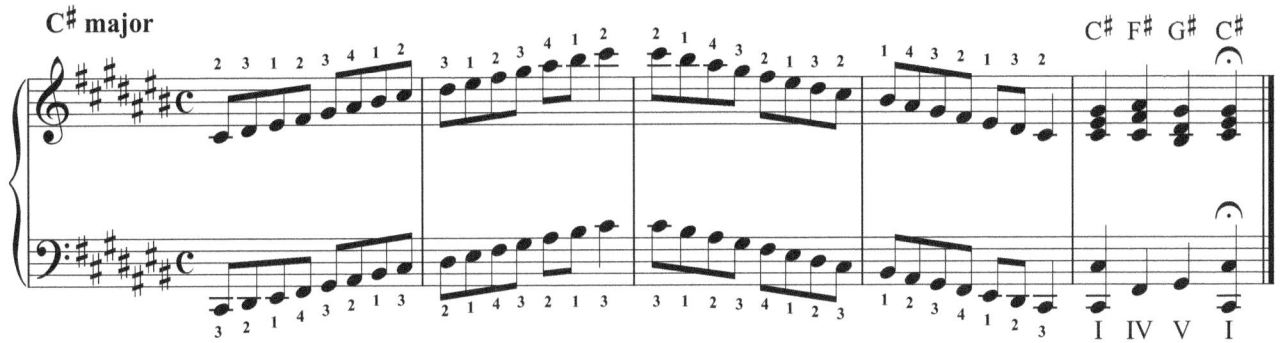

A# natural minor

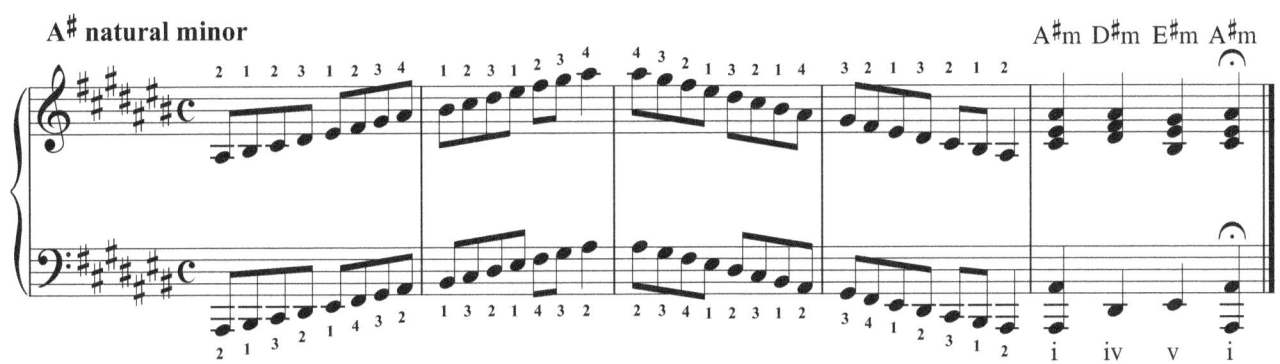

A# harmonic minor

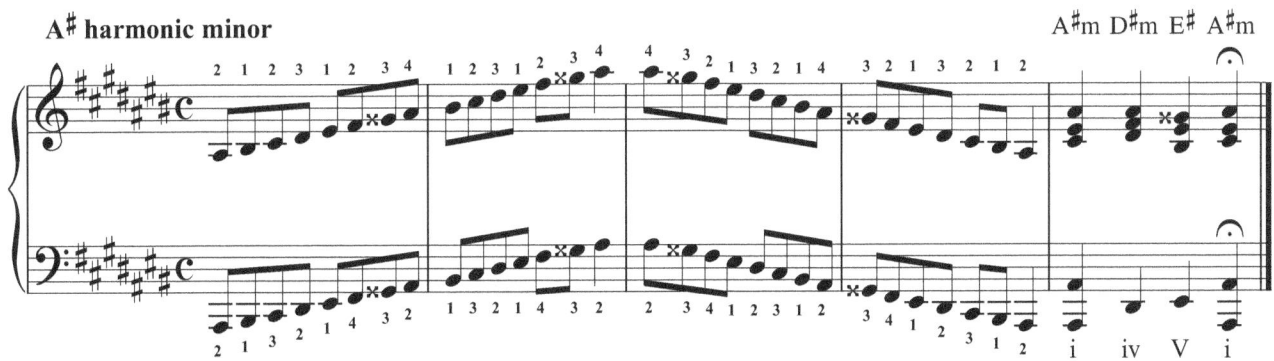

A# melodic minor

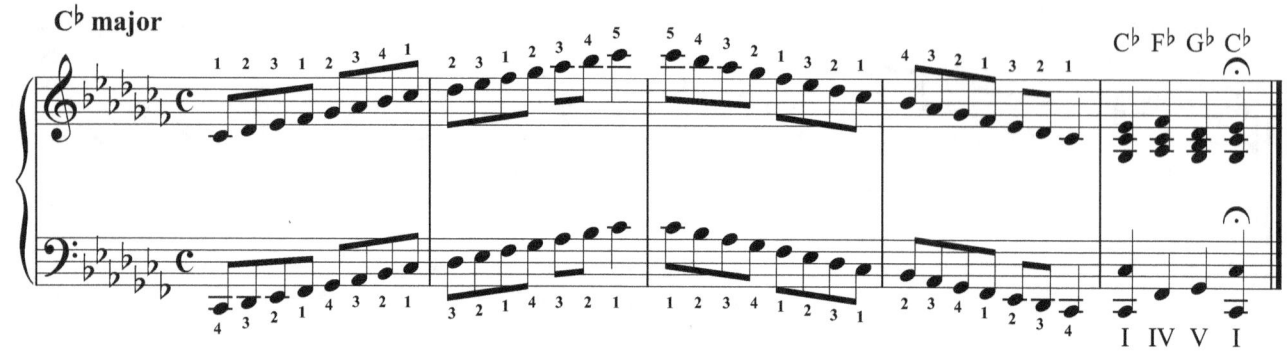
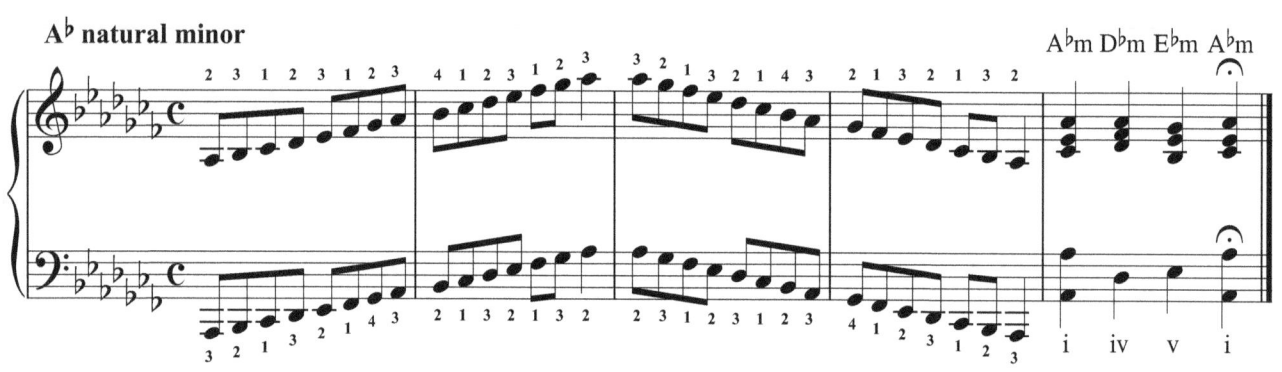
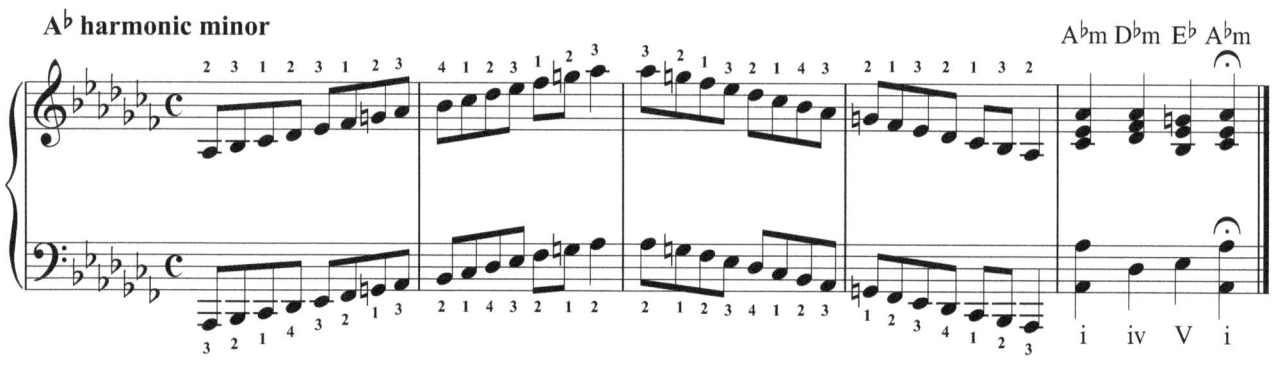

Chromatic scale

Traditional blues scale

Professional blues scale

177

Whole tone scales

Major Pentatonic scale

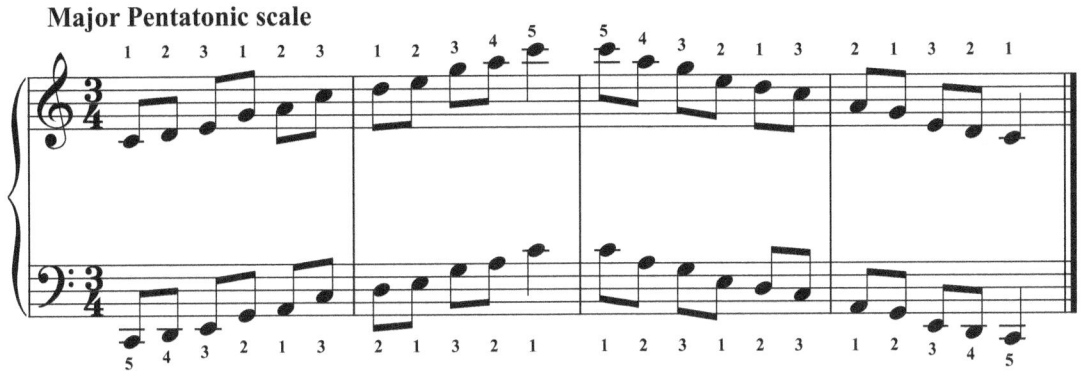

Minor Pentatonic scales

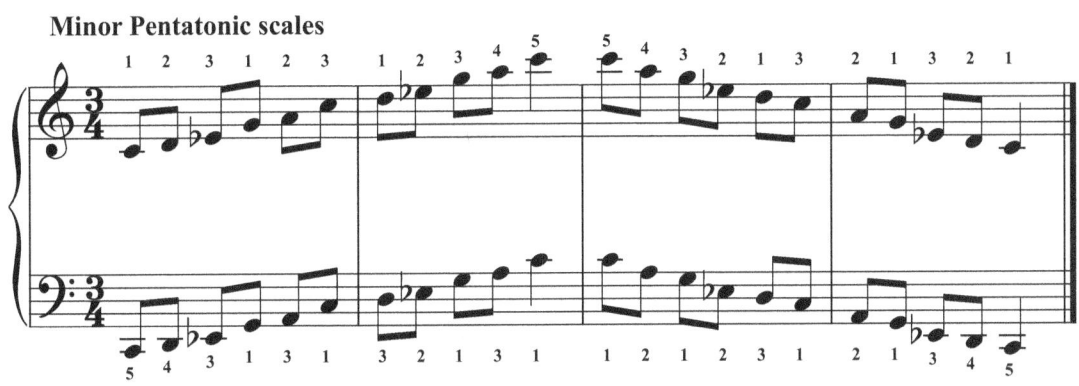

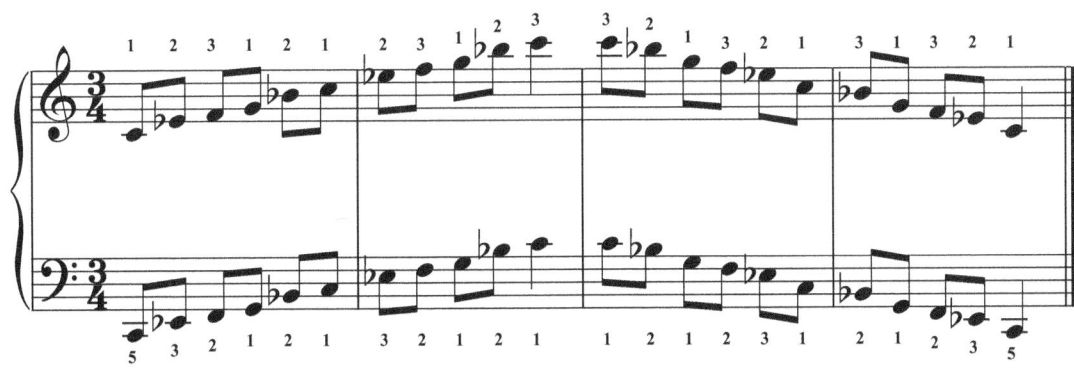

179

Appendix 2

More examples of time signatures

Remembering that in a time signature the top number represents how many beats there are in a bar of music and the bottom number tells what kind of a note gets one beat, there are time signatures that are less commonly seen but used for specific reasons, especially in older music.

The following Scandinavian melody in minor, bears an uncanny resemblance to patriotic songs from Britain and the United States.

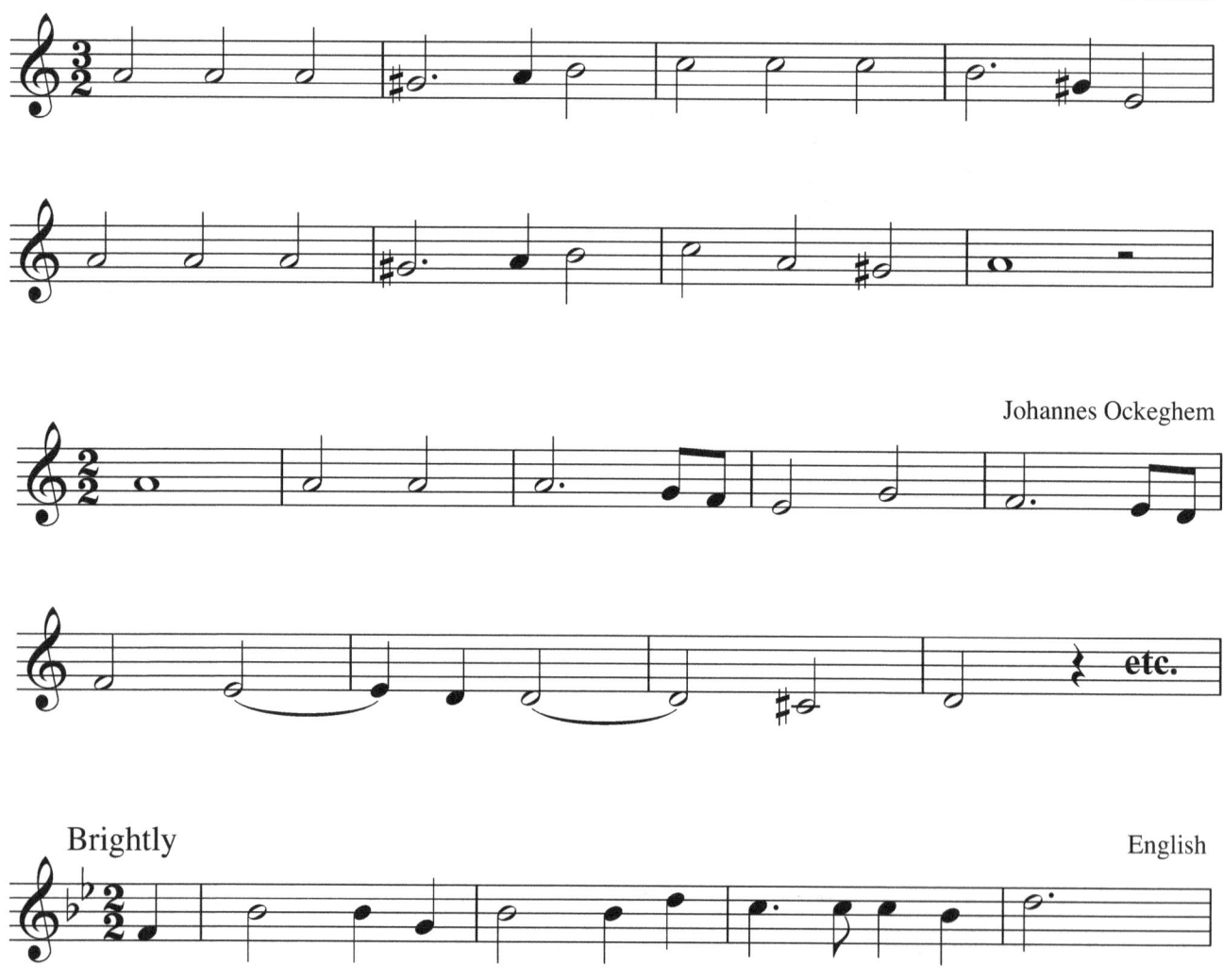

Here are more examples of how less-common time signatures are used.

GLOSSARY

Accent One of several types of symbols $>$ $\wedge$ $\triangle$ that indicate to play louder or more forcefully.

Accidental Symbols that raise, lower, negate or remind the player about half and whole step alterations in a melody or harmony. Examples of accidentals are sharps and double sharps, flats and double flats, and naturals.

Aeolian mode Another name for the natural minor scale.

Alberti bass Turning a three note chord into this rhythmic, repeating bass pattern: bottom note, top, middle, top.

Alto In four-part music, the voice below the soprano.

Anacrusis An upbeat or pickup.

Arpeggiate To play the notes of a chord consecutively rather than all at once. One can arpeggiate up or down.

Arpeggio A series of notes that are played consecutively.

Articulation A general term describing the way notes are to be played.

Augment To raise a note by a half step.

Authentic cadence The chord progression V – I or V – i.

Bar The more commonly used term for 'measure.'

Barline A short vertical line that separates bars.

Bass In four part music, the lowest voice or part. Also the name of a group of low-sounding instruments as in bass guitar, upright bass, bass trombone, bass drum.

Bass clef The lower pitched clef of the grand staff used for piano and other types of music.

Beam A straight or slanted horizontal line grouping eighth note values or greater.

Beat The pulse of music. Refers to both meter ($\frac{4}{4}$, $\frac{3}{4}$, etc.) and speed (tempo).

Bird's eye Musician slang for fermata.

Blues scale A beginner's tonal resources for improvising blues music: 1, ♭3, 4, ♭5, 5, ♭7. More advanced players add the 2nd, 6th, and major 3rd.

Bridge A departure or change-up in a song, sometimes giving another viewpoint.

Chart Music that can contain any of the following elements: chords, an individual melodic part, rhythmic figures, form indications, dynamics, articulations, lyrics or parts of lyrics, rehearsal numbers and rehearsal letters.

Chord In simplest form: three notes; a root, third and fifth.

Chord progression A series of chords that makes progress, that goes somewhere. A common chord progression from the 1950's was I-vi-IV-V-I.

Chord rocking The author's term for rocking back and forth between the two upper tones of a chord and its bottom note. The pattern John Lennon played to accompany himself in 'Imagine' could be considered a 'chord rocking' style.

Chorus Where the main idea of the song lies. Can contain the title.

Chromatic Using many or all of the following 12 notes appearing in half step relationships in a piece of music: C, C♯, D, D♯, E, F, F♯, G, G♯, A, A♯, B. The opposite of chromatic is diatonic.

Circle of Fifths A visual aid to understanding how many sharps or flats are contained in each major and minor key. Beginning at the top of a circle with C (no sharps or flats), moving clockwise by 5^{ths} produces the keys with sharps (G-D-A, etc.) Moving counterclockwise from C by 5ths produces the flat keys (F-B$\flat$-E$\flat$, etc.).

Clef A symbol on the leftmost side of the staff specifying a particular note as a reference point. The treble clef or G clef indicates the note G will be the second line from the bottom of the staff. The bass clef or F clef indicates that F will be the fourth line from the bottom.

Coda Literally 'tail' in Italian. The end section of the music.

Coda sign The symbol of a circle with a cross superimposed.

Common tone A note that two or more chords share. In the C chord (C-E-G) and the F chord (F-A-C) the common tone is the note C.

Compound meter When the essence of a time signature has more than one cycle of a pulse of '3.' $\frac{6}{8}$, $\frac{9}{8}$, and $\frac{12}{8}$ are examples of compound time. $\frac{3}{4}$ and $\frac{3}{8}$ are not.

Crescendo Gradually get louder. ⊏

Cut time Seeing music written in $\frac{4}{4}$ but thinking and interpreting in $\frac{2}{2}$; alla breve.

D.C. Da Capo A form direction to go back to the very beginning (the head).

Deceptive cadence A series of chords that seem to lead to the tonic (I) but end up on the submediant (vi).

Decrescendo Gradually become quieter. ⊐

Diatonic Of or pertaining to a major or minor scale.

Diminish To lower a note or notes by a half step.

Dominant The "five chord" (V) that functionally propels music back to the tonic.

Dorian mode Like a natural minor scale with a raised 6th.

Dot A tiny mark placed to the right of a note adding half the value of that note to the total duration.

Dotted half A half note with a dot to the right indicating 3 beats of duration.

Double flat A symbol ♭♭ meaning to lower a note by two half steps.

Double sharp A symbol 𝄪 meaning to raise a note by two half steps.

Doubling A compositional device where a voice or instrument takes the exact same part as another voice or instrument. "The left hand of the piano should be doubling the bass."

Downbeat The first beat of any bar. "Since there's no pickup, let's start at the downbeat of bar nine."

D.S. Dal Segno   A form direction to go to the sign. 𝄋

Dynamics Volume indications. "The dynamics of this section need to be quieter."

Eighth note triplet A musical device that imparts a feeling of '3' against a regular pulse of '2.' An eighth note triplet (three eighth notes) fits in the same time space as two regular eighth notes.

Eleventh A compound interval of an octave plus a perfect 4th. Also a chord technically made up of the 1st, 3rd, 5th, 7th, 9th and 11th but rarely voiced this way. More often the voicing is R-♭7-9-11.

Enharmonics The same note, named in two ways; F♯ and G♭, E♭♭ and D, A𝄪 and B are all enharmonics.

Fermata A symbol telling the player to hold the note he is on. Musician slang is 'bird's eye.' 𝄐

Fifth An interval consisting of three and a half steps.

Figure A group of notes, a short phrase. "Can I hear the figure at bar 8 again?"

Figured bass A notation system specifying bass notes and accompanying chords. Roman numerals indicate the chord and function while Arabic superscript numbers indicate the inversion. I V$^6_5$ I

Fingering The logical, thought-out process of deciding what fingers would be best to play a particular section of music.

First ending One or several bars of bracketed music that ends a first section.

First inversion A chord with the 3rd in the bass.

Flag A very short descending or ascending curved line added to a stem to give a single note a value of eighth, sixteenth, thirty-second or greater.

Flat A symbol ♭ that lowers a note by a half step.

Flat seven Also known as the 'subtonic.' In Mixolydian mode the 7th degree is flatted because it is a whole step away from the tonic. In a major scale the 7th degree, a half step away from the tonic, is the leading tone.

Flatted A note that has been lowered by a half step.

Footballs Musician slang for whole notes. "I want the synthesizer to play footballs."

Form Sections of music that together create a whole.

Fourth An interval consisting of two and a half steps.

Four four time The most frequently used time signature in popular music; also written as **C** and known as Common Time.

Function The job a chord performs. "The function of the V^7 is generally to lead back to the I."

Grace note A quickly played note.

Hairpin A slang term used in England meaning crescendo or decrescendo.

Half diminished Another way of indicating a minor 7 flat 5 chord. If you think of the chord in two halves – the triad and the 7th – the triad is diminished, the 7th is not. Ex: $A^{\varnothing 7}$

Half note An oval-shaped note plus stem indicating 2 beats of duration.

Half step Another way of describing a minor 2nd (m2).

Harmonic minor A scale using the formula WHWWHA2H.

Home key The author's term used to determine key signatures for modes. The home key of G Dorian is F, therefore G Dorian has one flat: $B^\flat$.

Hook A catchy phrase or sound.

Interval The distance between one note and another, usually measured to 13^{ths}.

Interval of transposition By what interval music is changed from one key to another. If a piece was in C and transposed to $E^\flat$, the interval of transposition would be a minor 3rd.

Improvisation Spontaneously making up your own music without writing it down.

Inversion Positioning the notes of a chord with reference to the lowest bass note; C-E-G is a root position C chord while E-G-C and G-C-E are inversions.

Key The tonal area of a piece of music; "Let's put that song in the key of F so it'll sound good when Britney and Lindsey sing it as a duet."

Key signature An arrangement of accidentals or nothing for the key of C following the clef sign indicating the tonality of the music.

Leading tone The 7th degree of the scale or the 7th chord (vii°) when it is a half step away from the tonic.

Lead sheet A simplified way of putting musical information on a page(s); may include title, chords, lyrics, melody or melodic figures, tempo, dynamics, articulations, form indications and symbols, bar numbers, section letters, author(s), arranger, copyright notice.

Ledger line A short, horizontal line placed either above or below the staff extending its range.

Legato A technique of playing music - usually melodies - that makes the notes sound connected; achieved by holding on to the previous note until the new note is played.

Lick A short musical idea or phrase. Also known as a riff. "Let's repeat the intro lick in the bridge."

Locrian A mode whose notes can be used to improvise over a minor 7 flat 5 chord. HWWHWWW.

Lowered Flatted; a note that has been dropped by a half step.

Lydian Like a major scale with a raised 4th.

Major scale Tones arranged as Whole, Whole, Half, Whole, Whole, Whole, Half.

Measure A short unit of time on a staff defined by bar lines on either side.

Mediant The 3rd in a series of 7 chords; one of four secondary triads.

Melodic minor A scale using the formula: WHWWWWH.

Meter The grouping of beats into usually equal measures.

Metronome A mechanical or electronic device that emits a controllable, steady pulse for practice purposes.

Middle C The note in the middle of the piano people use to orient themselves to the keyboard.

Mixolydian mode Like a major scale with a flatted 7th.

Modal Of or pertaining to a mode. "When I heard the progression Dm-F-G-C-Dm, I figured the piece was modal."

Mode A seven note arrangement of whole and half steps traced back to ancient civilizations.

Modulation The compositional process of changing keys.

Natural A symbol ♮ that reverses or neutralizes a sharped or flatted note.

Natural minor A scale using the formula WHWWHWW.

Ninth A compound interval of an octave plus a major 2nd. Also a chord made up in its entirety of the 1st, 3rd, 5th, 7th, and 9th.

Non-Harmonic tone A note or notes – possibly in the melody or part of the orchestration or accompaniment – that is not one of the chord tones. Ex: the note C sung or played against an E minor triad (E, G, B).

Note Can refer to either a key on the piano or other instrument, or the physical indication on staff paper of a musical pitch.

Octave The interval of six whole steps found as the first and last note of an 8 note diatonic scale.

Ostinato A repeating pattern or bass line. "Does the ostinato in 'Birthday' remind you a little of 'Oh, Pretty Woman?'"

Parallel fifths A series of notes all harmonized with a perfect fifth above or below. Used in Gregorian Chant, abandoned and forbidden in classical music, adopted and adored by pop, rock, blues, and jazz.

Parallel minor If you are in C major and you modulate to C minor, that is the parallel minor. The key signatures will be different.

Parallelism Harmonizing consecutive notes in the same way such as a melody of parallel 6^{ths} or a doubled bass line of parallel octaves.

Passing note A melody or accompaniment note that is not in the chord.

Pedal point See pedal tone.

Pedal tone A single bass note or octave played against a series of changing chords. In the progression C, F/C, G/C, C the pedal tone is C.

Pentachord The first five notes of a major or minor scale.

Pentatonic An ancient 5 note scale. Major pentatonic = 1, 2, 3, 5, 6, minor pentatonic = 1, $\flat$3, 4, 5, $\flat$7 or 1, 2, $\flat$3, 5, 6.

Phrase marks Curving arcs placed over music to indicate single ideas.

Phrygian mode Like a natural minor scale with a flatted 2nd.

Pickup The note(s) before the downbeat. Anacrusis.

Pitch The highness or lowness of sound. "Your piccolo is too high-pitched and shrill for this music. Try your flute."

Plagal cadence The chord progression IV – I. The sound of 'A-men.'

Primary chords The tonic (I or i), subdominant (IV or iv), and dominant (V or v) of any key.

Pulse Beat.

Quarter note A darkened note head plus stem indicating 1 beat of duration.

Quarter note triplet A musical device that imparts a feeling of '3' against a regular pulse of '2.' A quarter note triplet (three quarter notes) fits in the same time space as two regular quarter notes.

Raised A note that has been sharped or double sharped.

Relative major The key and scale located a minor 3rd above the relative minor.

Relative minor The key signature found a minor third below the relative major.

Range All the notes (from lowest to highest) a voice or instrument is capable of producing. Also, the lowest to highest notes of a melody.

Repeat sign Two vertical dots surrounding the middle line of the staff with a thin and thicker vertical line to the right or left indicating a section should be played again.

Répertoire The music a performer knows.

Rest One of a group of symbols indicating silence while a pulse continues.

Root The bass note that shares its name with the chord; in the chord of G made up of the notes G, B, D, the root is the note G.

Root position A chord in its most basic position where the chord name and the name of the bass note are the same.

Rhythm Short or long durations of sounds with or without accents, usually over a steady pulse either heard or felt.

Rhythmic figure A short characteristic phrase.

Ritard An indication to slow down. Abbreviated *Rit.*

Scalar Of or pertaining to a scale. "Since this melody by Bach ascends and descends the major scale exclusively, we could say it is both diatonic and scalar."

Scale An organized series of tones, usually made up of half and whole steps.

Second One of two intervals. A major 2nd (M2) consists of two half steps; the distance from D♭ to E♭ or F to G or B♭ to C. A minor 2nd (m2) is the distance from C to C♯ or E to F or B to C.

Secondary chords The supertonic (ii or ii°), mediant (iii, III or III⁺), submediant (vi, vi° or VI), and leading tone or subtonic chords (vii° or VII) of any key.

Secondary dominant The V^7 ("Five-seven") of any chord. To find the secondary dominant, go down a perfect fourth. The secondary dominant of Em is B^7. The secondary dominant of F♯ is C♯⁷.

Second ending One or several bars of bracketed music that take you into the next section. The second ending is almost always different in some ways from the first ending.

Second inversion A chord with the 5th in the bass.

Section letters Letters of the alphabet signifying specific sections of music that aid in quickly locating those sections during rehearsals. Also know as 'rehearsal letters.'

Seventh Can refer to the 7th degree of a scale, the interval of a major or minor 7th, or a major or dominant 7th chord. A major 7th interval (M7) is an octave minus a half step. A minor 7th interval (m7) is an octave minus a whole step.

Sharp A symbol ♯ that raises a note by a half step.

Sharped A note that has been raised by a half step.

Shortcut chord The author's definition of a chord name followed by a slash and the name of a bass note. Ex: F/G or C/B♭.

Sight reading The act of looking at a new piece of music and playing it.

Simple meter When the essence of a time signature has a pulse of '2.'

Sixth One of two intervals. A major 6th (M6) consists of a Perfect 5th plus a whole step. A minor 6th (m6) consists of a Perfect 5th plus a half step.

Soprano In four part music, the top voice.

Staccato A dot placed over a note indicating to play that note in a short, abrupt way.

Staff Five horizontal lines that serve as a grid on which to place notes for the purpose of writing music.

Steps Intervals that are either half or whole steps.

Subdominant The "four chord" (IV or iv).

Submediant The 6th in a series of 7 chords; one of four secondary triads.

Subtonic The flatted 7th degree of a scale or mode.

Supertonic The 2nd in a series of 7 chords; one of four secondary triads.

Syncopation A rhythm where weak beats are stressed or accented.

Take-down Either the process of transcribing music or the result.

Tenor In four part music, the voice above the bass.

Tempo The speed at which music is performed; "Let's take that at a much slower tempo - the trombone players are out of breath."

Tessitura The strongest part of a singer or instrumentalist's range.

Theory The ideas behind music: rhythm, melody, harmony, form, counterpoint, arranging, orchestration. Means the same as 'fundamentals.'

Third One of two intervals. A major 3rd (M3) consists of two whole steps. A minor 3rd (m3) consists of a step and a half.

Thirteenth A compound interval of an octave plus a major 6th. Also a chord containing a dominant 7th and the 13th.

Tie A short curved line connecting two notes of equal pitch. The total duration will be the sum of the two notes.

Time signature Two numbers that appear at the beginning of a piece of music. The top number tells how many beats there will be in one measure. The bottom number tells what kind of a note will get one beat.

Tonal Of a musical key.

Tonic The "one chord," (I). 'Home base' in terms of function and tonality.

Transpose To put music in a different key. "I need you to transpose that song up a half step."

Treble clef A symbol that gives specific meaning to the lines and spaces of the staff by referencing the second line from the bottom as the note G above middle C. Also known as the G clef.

Treble clef voicing Changing the position of tones in right hand chords to achieve different sounds; not to be confused with inversions that require bass notes.

Triad A three note chord: root, third, fifth.

Triplet A rhythmic grouping of three notes. See 'quarter note' or 'eighth note' triplet.

Tritone An interval composed of three whole steps such as F to B.

Turnaround The last bar or bars of a section of music that bring you back to the beginning of that section or leads you to another.

Upbeat The weak pickup note that precedes the strong downbeat. In the following example the word 'should' is the upbeat: "Should old acquaintance be forgot."

Verse The part of a song that sets forth the story or details.

Voicing Exchanging the positions of the notes of a chord. "Instead of voicing that chord C-E-G try G-C-E."

Voice Besides the sound a human being makes when singing or talking, a single musical line. "The inner voice needs to be on the major third."

Voice leading Writing a melody that follows specific classical rules such as 'the seventh of the V^7 chord should generally resolve downward to the 3rd of the I chord.'

Whole note An oval-shaped note indicating 4 beats of duration.

Whole step Another way of describing a major 2nd (M2).

Whole tone scale A 6 note scale consisting of all whole tones: WWWWWW.

INDEX

A

anacrusis 81
arpeggiation 153
augmented
  fourth 122
  interval 122

B

Bach, J.S.
  chorale bass 115-118
  melody 118-120
bar 4
bass clef 11
bass lines 4
B flat major
  chords 133, 146
  relative minor of
    scale 133
beaming 112
beat 4
bonus notes 134

C

chart 92
chord
  function 89
  major
    formula for 89
  primary 88
  symbols 88
chromatic 63
  scale 64
circle of fifths 123
C major
  chords 88, 89
  scale 41-43, 45, 46
compound meter 140
counting 5, 111, 113
circle of fifths 123, 125
  diagram 126

D

diatonic 65
diminished
  fifth 122
D major
  chords 129
  scale 128
  primary triads 129
dominant 90
dot 36
dotted half
  note 36
  rest 80
dotted quarter
  note 113
  rest 113
downbeat 81
durations 1
Dylan, Bob 90

E

eighth
  note 110
  rest 112
enharmonic 126

F

fingering 9, 98
finger substitution 130
flag 112
flat
  symbol 23, 63
Flight of the
  Bumble Bee 65
F major
  chords 91
  scale 74
four four time 4
fourth
  augmented 122
  perfect 122
function 89
fundamentals 40

G

G clef 2
G major
  chords 91, 92
  scale 66, 67
grand staff 15

H

half
  note 3
  rest 80
  step 40
hand position 7
how to construct
  major scale 41
  major chord 89

I

interval 40

J

Jingle Bells
  almost 6

K

key signature 66
keyboard notes 2

L

ledger line 3
legato 153

M

major
  quality 88
  scale 41
  second 40, 121
  third 87, 121
measure 4
meter
  compound 140-141
  simple 139

middle C
  finding 2
minor
  second 40, 121
  third 87, 121
mnemonics 23

N

Nashville Number System 94
natural 65
  symbol 65
note 2
notehead 78

O

octaves 11

P

Pachelbel's Canon 73
perfect
  fifth 122
  fourth 122
piano (instrument) 1, 2
piano skills
  benefits of 21
pickup 81
pitch 1
practicing 23
  how to 21
primary triads 88
  major 89
progression 90

Q

quarter
  note 3
  rest 80

R

repeat sign 81

rests
  dotted half 80
  half 80
  quarter 80
  whole 80
rhythm 1

S

scales 45
seating position 7
second
  major 40
  minor 40
semitone 40
shapes
  recognizing 24, 25
sharp 23, 63
sight reading 26
  eye path 25
simple
  duple 139
  meter 139
  quadruple 140
  triple 140
staff 2
  grand 15
stem direction 78, 112
subdominant 90

T

tessitura 90
third
  major 87
  minor 87
three-four time 82
thumb under 42
tie 79
time signature 4
tonic 89
triads 88
transpose
  chords 91, 92
  melodies 91
treble clef 2
tritone 123

U

upbeat 81

V

voicings
  triad 92

W

waltz 82
whole
  note 3
  rest 80, 84
  step 40
  tone 40

E   D   C

B   A   G   F

F   E   D   C

C   B   A   G

```
A         B         C

D         E         F         G

G         A         B         C

C         D         E         F
```

F   G   A   B

G   F   E   D

                                A

www.ingramcontent.com/pod-product-compliance
Lightning Source LLC
Chambersburg PA
CBHW081215230426
43666CB00015B/2744